THE HAPPINESS PATHWAY

WHEN LIFE UNRAVELS,
WEAVE YOURSELF
A SOFTER KIND OF JOY.

CHARU MOORJANI

ISBN: 978-1-7645019-0-3

To my younger self:

'Dear little one, you are enough, and your happiness will grow the moment you stop trying to be someone else to fit in.'

ACKNOWLEDGEMENT

This book is the truest reflection of a journey I never thought I would be brave enough to put into words. This section, which I wrote at the very end of the process was the most fun part of the book to write, as it reminded me how much love and support I am surrounded by in this life. I am humbled and thrilled to know that each and every word in this book has been shaped by the people and experiences I've had in my life. While the pages carry my story, they also bear the imprints of so many people who have shaped, supported and loved me along the way.

To my late father, your absence has shaped me as much as your presence once did. I still carry your lessons in my heart: to stay curious, to rise above every fall and to believe in possibilities. There are moments in this book where I wrote as if I were speaking to you, hoping that somehow you could read between the lines. I hope I've made you proud.

To my late grandmother (or Moni-Mumma as I called you), your stories, your resilience in the face of loss and the quiet grace with which you rebuilt a life from nothing have been guiding lights for me. You taught me that abundance isn't wealth; it's the spirit within you to continue living your life fully even in your last moments.

To my mother, thank you for being my anchor. Even in the moments when life has felt impossibly heavy, your quiet strength reminds me that I am never truly alone. The love that you don't share openly, but which I know is always silently there, is a constant in my life.

To my brother, Tanuj, thank you for always being my home. Thank you for the laughter that lightens the darkest seasons, the calls that remind me of who I am and the way you always stand firmly by my side without ever needing to be asked. Thank you for inspiring me to always reinvent myself. I couldn't have found the motivation to write these chapters without your steady presence and inspiration.

To my partner, my love Adrian, thank you for showing me that love can be gentle, safe and freeing; for holding space for my dreams; for celebrating every small win; and for reminding me that creating happiness is simple, real and possible every day. You've been both my home and my compass in this new chapter of my life. This book carries fragments of the life we've built together… the quiet mornings, the long conversations, the time spent in nature, the shared laughter and the moments when your belief in me was stronger than my own. You've taught me that a relationship doesn't have to be a battle for survival but a sanctuary for growth. Thank you for reminding me that vulnerability can coexist with strength and that true partnership is not about completing one another but about walking side by side, hand in hand, as we each grow into who we are meant to be.

To my little baby, TimTam, thank you for teaching me what unconditional love truly looks like. Your warm kisses, wagging tail and boundless joy remind me every single day that happiness can be found in the simplest moments and that love needs no words.

To all my dearest friends, you know who you are. Thank you for listening to the messy parts of my story, for holding me in my vulnerability and for reminding me of my own strength when I doubted it the most. Thank you for being mirrors when I couldn't see myself clearly, for gently calling me back when I strayed too far from my truth and for teaching me that chosen family can be just as powerful and healing as the family we are born into. Your laughter, dinner dates, late-night talks over wine and unwavering presence are reminders that connection is one of the purest forms of happiness.

To my editor, Heather, thank you for believing in this book and pushing me to go deeper, to write not just what was safe but what was true.

And finally to you, my dear reader, thank you for picking up this book. My hope is that in these words you find not just my story but fragments of your own. May this happiness pathway remind you that happiness is not a single destination but a way of being, one that you are worthy of every day.

With love and endless gratitude,

Charu

CONTENTS

THE HAPPINESS PATHWAY

CHARU MOORJANI

My quest for happiness: A personal journey

I STOOD IN the kitchen with the aroma of freshly brewed coffee surrounding me like a warm hug, yet beneath this heavenly scent festered an undeniable sense of emptiness. The morning sunlight filtered through the window lighting up the room in a false display of peacefulness that sharply contrasted with the storm developing within me. Across the room stood my now ex-husband, his back turned, while he busily scrolled through his phone. He seemed oblivious to the internal chaos that had become my constant friend. To the outside world, we seemed like the perfect couple, with our social media photos showing gleaming smiles, date nights, holidays, as well as the significant milestones we had achieved together, such as buying a home. However, behind closed doors, the love and bond that once held us close had worn into a soulless existence.

In that moment while watching him completely absorbed in his phone, an overwhelming sense of unhappiness came over me. *Is this what my life is all about?*

That artificial mask of happiness appeared so thin and fragile, with an inner life carved from loneliness and longing.

And knowing it made me angry, leaving a bitter taste of dissatisfaction that I had bottled up for far too long. *How is it that I can feel so hollow inside when everyone around me perceives me as successful and content in life?*

To seek clarity, I impulsively looked to my parents for answers. It's common to rely on the familiar family template you have known since childhood when facing uncertainty in life. It was then that it hit me. I realised my life had become a mirror of their life. A marriage characterised by mere co-existence, devoid of emotional connection and shaped by society's expectations. In that moment, my entire life collapsed like a sandcastle against the tide. I didn't want to live my life the same way they had, quietly struggling through every day, every year. I needed to reclaim my life and find my own path to discover what happiness meant for me, even if it meant taking a few steps backward to unlearn everything I knew.

Before this significant moment of realisation, I had always safely hidden behind a cautiously curated identity that was acceptable to everyone. As a daughter, wife, friend and employee, my achievements on the outside were easy to see and very impressive, marked by promotions at work, financial growth and admiration from peers. Internally, however, I was drowning in discontent. The simple act of getting out of bed in the morning was becoming heavier and more burdensome. Each interaction with peers, family and friends felt more superficial than the one before, leaving me desperate for deeper connections. Despite all these external validations, the things that were supposed to bring me happiness started to feel empty and useless.

To fully understand my journey and perhaps your own, I feel I need to share a little bit more about where I began.

I was born in Delhi, India, into a small nuclear family by Indian standards. Both my parents were hardworking professionals from modest backgrounds, who were determined to build a better life for their kids. My grandma lived with us, or perhaps it's more accurate to say we (my dad, mum, my younger brother and I) lived with her. This is something that is woven into the fabric of Indian culture. For the first few years of my life, my dad's younger sister lived with us as well, until she married. We shared a tiny two-bedroom apartment. It was chaotic, loud and bursting with clashing personalities; yet, in between the storms, there were snippets of warmth, humour and love.

I don't have many memories from my childhood, which is something that once troubled me deeply. I wondered why so much of my early life was a blur to me, but over time, I've learned to make peace with it. Working on myself to heal my childhood wounds has taught me that some memories return when you're ready, while others remain hidden forever. I've also discovered that my mind tends to release anything older than five years, so for me, journalling and taking way too many photos and videos has become my way of keeping my memory alive and preserving pieces of my story. Much of this book is built from those journals, both handwritten and digital, as well as photos and videos that capture moments my memory could not hold onto.

Growing up I always felt like I was the odd one out in my family. The only person I felt truly connected to was my younger brother. As a child, I used to fantasise that another family would one day come forward and reveal that I had been accidentally swapped at the hospital because surely that would explain the disconnect I felt in my own home.

Ours was a typical middle-class household with working parents who had chaotic schedules. There were occasional family game nights, but also explosions of temper kids should never have to witness. I won't go into the darkest stories as they belong to a different chapter and perhaps another book, but they left marks that shaped how my brother and I bonded. We formed an unspoken pact to rise above the patterns we grew up in and to build better lives, healthier relationships and kinder futures for ourselves.

I worked hard in school driven by an ambition I couldn't yet understand, fuelled partly by pain and partly by hope. I earned good grades, got into a reputable college, and it was then that I met my ex-husband. We dated for a while, but when he planned to move to Australia to study, we decided to part ways. Life, however, had other plans. Within a year, I too found myself boarding a flight to Australia to study and be close to him.

My uni years in Sydney are a bit of a blur for me, and I can now acknowledge that they were shaped by emotional overwhelm. It was my first time alone in a foreign country and it was then that he became my anchor. I didn't realise it at the time, but I had slipped into deep co-dependency. When his very traditional Indian family began pressuring him to get married, I clung to the idea of a fairytale wedding and future with him. At 22, I said yes and at 23 I stood at the altar: naïve, sheltered and utterly unaware of who I truly was and what I wanted from my life.

The wedding itself was far from a fairytale; it was stressful, suffocating and filled with unrealistic expectations that I did not understand. Then came the honeymoon, planned entirely according to his desires without any consideration for mine. We went to Macau instead of the originally intended Maldives, so he could spend more time with his family in India after the wedding.

On the first night I fell severely ill. Looking back now, I believe my body had finally rebelled before my mind would admit the truth, that I was going through with a marriage I did not believe in. I had wanted to call it off at the last minute but didn't, due to my fear of what people would think.

Within days, my lungs collapsed. I was diagnosed with Guillain Barré syndrome (GBS) and spent a month in the ICU in Macau on a mechanical ventilator, fighting for my life. My full recovery within a year was considered rare and almost miraculous.

This was the first turning point of my adult life, one that shook me to my core.

My ex-husband supported me through my recovery, and I will always be grateful for that. But within six months of regaining my strength and seven months into my marriage, I realised I had made a mistake. The man I married was not the same man I had known while dating as a young adult. I had been too naïve, too blinded by my desire for a fairytale, to see what stood in front of me.

For years, I held onto the guilt about him having stood by me during my illness and how leaving would make me seem ungrateful. I tried to endure the emotional shifts, the inconsistent behaviour and the growing disconnection. It took nearly four years for the truth to crystalise that this life I was living was not aligned with who I was or who I wanted to be.

And so the journey to find myself and the meaning of happiness began… with the bold and difficult step of ending my unhappy marriage. It was not an easy farewell, but a bumpy and agonising separation riddled with emotional turbulence and the burden of judgement from society. I felt critiqued and isolated, yet in the midst of this mess I experienced a sense of liberation. It wasn't easy, but this chaos felt like I was finally escaping a cage I had been living in my whole life. This was how I learned to trust my gut and strip away who I used to be, a blind follower of family and society in contrast to the person I truly am, hidden away inside.

This journey was filled with obstacles, moments of self-doubt and times of moving around in the dark, but gradually I started to find my true self. I started to develop my own pace in life slowly. I don't think I achieved continuous happiness, but perhaps that's not the point. What did happen was that I slowly started to feel alive again. I learned to prioritise and recognise what resonated with me and my soul rather than blindly following the prescribed life path that everyone is expected to follow. I was the healthiest I had ever been in my life, focused on fitness and self-care. My career soared and grew stronger, reaching new heights driven by real passion and purpose. I grew to love travelling and exploring new places. In this newfound freedom and search for happiness, I met my current partner who is a real source of support, kindness and love. Life became more balanced, happy and directed towards my soul.

Then came an unexpected turning point in my life, the passing of my father. He had suffered from Parkinson's disease from the early age of 30 after a severe head injury. This event impacted my family and our life profoundly. During my younger years, I was a daddy's girl; however, our relationship became strained and complicated during my teenage years, as I first started being drawn into my parents' arguments and forced to pick sides.

Our relationship was further distanced by my migration to Australia and had further deteriorated alongside his health over the years. His passing brought an overwhelming wave of guilt and grief, forcing me to look inward more. I started questioning everything in my life. Why was I seeking superficial success, living a superficial life filled with superficial connections and not prioritising what was most important to me? Losing him forced me to face myself, peeling away layers of fear and anxiety about accepting the suffocating changes I knew I had to embrace.

Soon after, the COVID-19 pandemic added fuel to my emotional struggles. The forced lockdown sent me into depression and those previously healthy parts of my life, i.e. health, work and relationships, began to break down under this mounting burden. Even though I was now in a loving relationship, there was still an emptiness within me that indicated happiness wasn't necessarily situational but rather a deeply rooted part of my thought process and mental state.

Determined yet cautious, I started my journey of self-discovery and healing. I tried a lot of things, e.g. learning reiki healing and going on a healing journey myself. However, in the end, mindset tools were what resonated with me most. I went on to study mindset coaching, which helped me shape a plan for myself on this transformative journey I was on. Small but powerful mindfulness practices became the foundation of my days, transforming everyday routines into profound experiences of gratitude and presence. I stumbled upon biohacking and incorporated some of the simpler practices, which allowed me to uncover a more vibrant and dynamic individual beneath the layers of fatigue that had built up. Further, learning to enjoy my own company and the power of solitude unlocked strengths within me that I did not know I had.

Yet, the path to healing is rarely direct or linear. Old childhood wounds unexpectedly came to the surface, requiring me to find inner courage and self-compassion, a skill I found much harder to develop than any job or professional skills. What I learned was the importance of setting boundaries in any relationship, be it with family, friends, co-workers or romantic partners. Initially, these steps were uncomfortable and required a lot of courage, but ultimately, they were very liberating.

Every time you say 'no' to something that doesn't align with your soul or let go of a toxic relationship, it becomes an affirmation of self-worth. Each step toward healthier boundaries is a step toward emotional clarity and inner empowerment. Each difficulty I experienced in this process of self-discovery taught me something new, and each win reaffirmed my commitment to authenticity and staying true to who I am.

Discovering the principle of abundance mindset reprogrammed my mind. It helped me replace my limiting beliefs, stemming from old fears, with gratitude for every aspect of life on a daily basis. As a result, my working life gained a new purpose, fulfilling relationships blossomed, and bliss became within reach, real and personal.

This book is the result of my journey of self-discovery and my desire to share my story. Not just to heal myself, but to offer hope and direction to anyone who may be feeling stuck in life, facing their own struggles or grappling with that empty feeling inside. In it, I share details from my journey to demonstrate how genuine happiness can be cultivated amid life's chaos, and offer practical insights and exercises you can use to illuminate your own path forward to achieve a happy and fulfilling life.

As you read through these pages, I invite you to join me on this journey and reflect deeply on your own path to finding and nurturing a happiness that is uniquely your own, one that can guide and support you through life's inevitable challenges. This is by no means a prescription where you take a pill and get cured, nor is it a one-size-fits-all solution for cultivating happiness. Rather, it is a reflection upon the journey of self-discovery that I have taken, along with the mindset tools that helped me and that I now offer to you.

Join me in experiencing The Happiness Pathway.

PART 1

UNDERSTANDING HAPPINESS

CHAPTER 1

What does happiness really mean?

As I SAT down to write this book, I began reflecting on an old but familiar question that had repeatedly emerged throughout my life and had quietly evolved over the years.

What does happiness mean?

When I was younger, this seemed like a very easy question, and the answer was always clear and simple. Happiness, as I believed at that time, was always linked to external achievements, a belief that felt quite consistent with my upbringing. If I earned the right degree, secured a well-paid, prestigious job, and built a picture-perfect life carefully crafted to meet societal expectations while mirroring the glossy ideals of success portrayed in magazines and movies, I would finally grasp that elusive feeling of contentment and happiness that seemed to dance just out of reach. It was a solid belief for me at the time, and it gave me something to chase after. And chase I did.

I ran headlong into ambition, chasing after material success and ticking off milestones like a checklist I had to complete to attain happiness. I love a checklist, as the people who are close to me know well. I create lists for everything, both in my personal and professional life. So for me, ticking off a checklist for happiness seemed very aligned: the right degree, a well-paying job, a fancy car, a house in the right part of the city, designer handbags and outfits, a large social circle, the photos of milestone moments framed and shared all over the socials. And yet behind the carefully constructed façade, I felt an emptiness that could not be filled.

On my graduation day I stood amidst a sea of caps and gowns, surrounded by people celebrating. There was pride on each face, there was laughter, and there was a bright future waiting ahead of us. But in my mind, there was also a sense of detachment, as if I were an actor in my own life. I grinned for the camera, posed for pictures with my degree, and tossed my cap into the air in triumph, but the happiness was muted and almost false. A similar sensation accompanied me into my first big promotion. Colleagues toasted my success. I wore the title like a badge. But when the noise settled and the congratulations faded, I found myself asking, *Why doesn't this feel like enough?*

Learning to let go of the old narrative

What I realised, very slowly, quietly and almost invisibly, was that the happiness I was chasing had been conditioned into me. It was something I picked up from my family, society and everyone I saw around me. It was something that was always out of reach and never enough. It was always conditional, with the feeling that if I achieved something, then I would be happy. But as soon as I achieved the goal, I felt like the finish line kept shifting and moving further away and out of reach again. The more I acquired, the more intangible happiness became. And what was worse was that I had bought into the narrative that it was my fault for not feeling satisfied.

I hadn't worked hard enough. I hadn't achieved enough. I hadn't become enough.

It took a long time and a series of unremarkable yet quietly profound moments to help me unlearn this narrative: a slow afternoon walking on an empty beach with the breeze carrying the taste of salt and seagulls claiming the shore while whispering their secrets; laughter shared over a glass of wine with a friend whose presence felt like home; the calm satisfaction of finishing a creative project unrelated to work or being paid. These simple moments, so easily overlooked, held a depth and intensity that grand milestones never had. The joy of those basic moments pointed me in the right direction and it was then that I began to realise the truth. Happiness is not something we achieve. It's something we create.

This shift marked the beginning of me changing my mindset from chasing happiness to creating it. It wasn't a sudden shift, nor was it easy; rather it was a gradual change and it took a lot of effort not to hold on to the narrative I had grown up with my whole life. When I started discussing these ideas with friends and family, I learned that many of us have been raised on the myth that happiness is a destination.

Like scaling a mountain peak, we arrive at the summit after a strenuous hike. We are taught that happiness is circumstantial and tethered to success, wealth, beauty or relationships. And perhaps most dangerously we're conditioned to believe that happiness means always being upbeat and that negative emotions should be avoided, silenced or overcome.

However, real happiness, as I've come to understand, is far more convoluted and much more generous. It doesn't require that we be constantly cheerful. It doesn't hinge on flawless circumstances. Instead it invites us to be present. To know ourselves. To live in alignment with our core values even when the world tells us to chase something else. It's not about relentless positivity; it's about authenticity.

For me, happiness in its truest form is a state of being, rooted in purpose, self-awareness and the ability to find meaning even in the midst of life's inevitable chaos. It develops not from having 'the perfect life' but from cultivating a life that feels true to yourself.

Pleasure vs. fulfilment

One of the most liberating realisations I've had lately is understanding the distinction between pleasure and fulfilment. Pleasure is wonderful but momentary, like an exquisite meal, a pleasing compliment or an exciting purchase. It sparkles and lights us up for the moment and then fades away like a shooting star leaving us hungry for more, to have that dopamine hit again. Fulfilment, on the other hand is quieter, but more long lasting. It grows from connections, creativity and contribution, and it gives us a sense of inner harmony. It fills our souls in a way that pleasure never could. And it's in fulfilment that I've found a deeper and more sustainable form of happiness.

For me, fulfilment comes through creating but not for recognition or income, just for the pure joy of expressing myself. It comes in reconnecting with my body through dancing and yoga. In sharing stories that might help others feel less alone. In learning to love my own company without needing an audience.

So I want to invite you, to pause and reflect today. What does happiness mean to you? Is it shaped by your own truths or by expectations of others? Are your goals leading you close to joy or further from it with a goal for happiness that is ever shifting? What moments in your life have felt most real? Where you felt most alive, the most 'YOU'?

These are not easy questions. But they are essential ones.

As we move forward in this exploration together, I hope you'll consider letting go of the outdated narratives. Happiness is not a race. It is not a trophy. It is not found in applause or awards. It is found in presence. In alignment. In the brave and beautiful act of living a life that is true to yourself.

Let this be the beginning of a more expansive, grounded and deeply personal experience of joy. One that does not require chasing but rather brings you home to yourself.

Use the exercises on the next couple of pages to help you get started with your own happiness journey.

PRACTICAL EXERCISES FOR STARTING YOUR HAPPINESS JOURNEY

1. Define your happiness

Take out a journal or use this space to write your personal definition of happiness.

Reflect on the following questions:

- What does happiness look like for me, not my family, not society, just me?
- When was the last time I felt truly happy, and what made that moment meaningful?
- If I removed external approval (likes, praise, validation), what would still feel fulfilling?

I have included a snippet of my journal here to give you an idea of how easy and simple it can be:

Happiness for me means waking up with a sense of peace and purpose. It's not about my job or what I do for work, it's about knowing that how I spend my time reflects what matters to me. One of the happiest moments I can recall was a quiet morning walk by the beach, with no agenda just the sound of waves and the warmth of the sun. Even without anyone watching, I felt whole. Knowing that it makes me happy doing this, I make sure I start my day slow, with a cup of coffee, walking along the beach enjoying the sound of waves.

Write your thoughts below:

2. Joy compass mapping

The life quadrant

Draw in your own journal or use the quadrant below to answer the following questions:

- What are the moments I have felt most alive?
- What are the moments I have felt drained or lost?
- Who are the people who light me up?
- Who are the people who dim my light?

Here is a snippet from my journal to get your brain juices flowing:

Moments I felt most alive	Moments I felt drained or lost
Impromptu solo trip to London Family holiday spending quality time with each other	Endless meetings without meaning Being stuck with people who constantly complain or are stuck in victim mentality
People who light me up My partner My dog My Brother My friends	**People who dim my light** A friend who constantly complains A family member who constantly competes Fake niceness

Use the space below to write or sketch your quadrant in your journal and reflect on patterns that emerge.

Moments I felt most alive	Moments I felt drained or lost

People who light me up	People who dim my light

3. The 'should' detox

List five things you currently do or pursue because you think you 'should'.

Beside each, answer:

- Who told me I should do this?
- Does this still align with who I am or want to be?

Here is one 'should' from my journal:

Running a side hustle

Who told me? **Social media hustle culture.**

Alignment? **Not right now, it's burning me out.**

Use the table below to complete your reflections:

1.
Who told me?
Alignment?

2.
Who told me?
Alignment?

3.
Who told me?
Alignment?

4.
Who told me?
Alignment?

5.
Who told me?
Alignment?

4. Presence practice

Practise 'pause and notice' for a whole day:

- Before any major task or interaction, take a 10-second pause.
- Ask yourself: Am I present? Am I aligned with how I want to feel today?

Pro tip: If you are struggling with being present try this below simple awareness exercise:

Pick any mundane task you do on a daily basis. Speak to yourself while doing the task. I know it sounds odd, but it's the simplest way of bringing your awareness back to the present.

As an example, I have listed the steps I take to make a coffee. To bring my awareness to the present instead of doing this task in auto mode, I say the following statements while I am making my coffee:

'I am taking the cup out of the cupboard.'

'I am turning the coffee machine on.'

'I am putting milk in the machine.'

'I am waiting for the coffee to be poured in my cup.'

'I am holding my coffee feeling the warmth in my hands ready to drink it now.'

Reflect at the end of the day in your journal or use the space below:

What did you notice?

How did this shift impact your experience of happiness?

Notes:

ON A FINAL NOTE

As you complete this chapter and related practice exercises, I know you won't have all the answers right away, but I hope you are walking away with curiosity.

Curiosity about yourself.

Curiosity about the stories you've been told and the ones you're ready to rewrite.

Curiosity about the kind of life that makes you feel alive, one that feels less like a performance and more like peace.

You don't need to have it all figured out. You just need to start listening to yourself, to your joy, your trust, your breath.

Because maybe happiness isn't something to find. Maybe it's something to come home to.

Let that thought sit with you…

Then keep going.

CHAPTER 2

The science and spirit of happiness

For years, I moved through life according to an unspoken script, graduating with honours, landing the right job, curating a social circle that looked good on paper. On the outside, I appeared successful. But success, I would come to learn, is a brittle substitute for meaning.

I floated through conversations like a ghost in a crowded room. Dinners, brunches and celebrations all blurred into a carousel of rehearsed interactions. 'How's work?' 'Have you seen the new Netflix series?' These were the lines we all knew, spoken with familiar cadence but empty resonance. I became skilled at impersonating someone who was content. It was a performance mastered over time, admired many times, but never true to what I felt beneath the surface.

Underneath, an unspoken question thudded more vigorously with every passing day:

Is this what happiness is supposed to feel like?

The illusion of fulfilment

Much of our culture confuses accomplishment and happiness. We're taught as children to define ourselves by external markers like career success, relationship status and possessions. I did all of it 'correctly' but in pursuing those markers, I lost sight of something more important… myself.

I was not alone. Positive psychology studies have long proven that the correlation between success, money and happiness plateaus after a certain level. Emotional well-being increases with income up to about $75,000 per annum, after which the gains disappear, according to a Princeton University study.

Higher income is neither a path to reported happiness nor a means to escape unhappiness or stress, even though it still boosts people's life evaluations. Those deeper sources of happiness, such as connection, purpose and autonomy can't be purchased or checked off a list. They must be cultivated. But cultivating them requires honesty. And honesty can be terrifying.

Breaking the script

For me, the crisis arrived not with some life-changing turn of events, but with a progressive breaking down. Friendships that had once been lively became tense. 'Let's catch up soon,' we'd assure one another, fully knowing we wouldn't. The security of shared experiences no longer compensated for the absence of emotional intimacy. I realised how often I bent myself into versions of who I thought others wanted me to be.

It was simpler to perform than to disappoint. But something inside me craved authenticity. I wanted to have genuine relationships, not obligatory ones. For comforting quiet, not suffocating. For presence, not performance.

Then came the event that shook me so deeply, and change became inevitable… my father passed away. The loss was seismic, but so was the silence that followed. I still remember the flight back home to India from Australia and the ache in my chest that no distraction could cure. I stared blankly at the in-flight map to track my journey across the ocean, a thousand memories flooding in with every passing hour. I knew I wasn't just flying home; I was flying towards an irreversible loss and a home that would never feel the same.

When I arrived, I stood frozen by my parents' door and saw my dad's lifeless body. The man who had raised me, protected me, lectured me, loved me, now just a body in a room filled with sorrow.

The funeral was deeply emotional, a ritual that spanned 13 days after the cremation, as is the tradition in India. The house was filled with relatives, neighbours, friends and well-wishers offering condolences wrapped in memories. But then the last garland wilted and the last guest left, it was just us: my mother, my brother and me. Three people sitting in the vastness of that house, surrounded by colossal absence. The silence was deafening. It felt like an entire chapter of my life had ended suddenly without any warning.

And in that suspended moment between presence and absence, a flood of questions rushed in:

Had he truly lived? Or did he also follow a script? Was he genuinely happy or just better at pretending?

And if a life can end so suddenly, what is it meant to be?

These questions clung to me like the Delhi smog outside my window. I tried to replay the fragments of his days in my head. The family boardgame nights, the road trips, the loud laughter over cold beer at family gatherings. He seemed so alive in those memories rooted in simplicity and connection. But now, faced with his absence, I couldn't help but wonder, *Was that enough? Is that all happiness really is?*

I thought of my father's long hours of work, the sacrifices he made, the structure and routine he followed. He had done everything 'right' and built a life of stability and duty. But...

Was it his life? Or was it just a version he had been taught to live by his parents and society?

And more importantly: *Was I doing the same?*

The grief didn't just break me open, it demanded I take a hard look at how I'd been living. Because if life could slip away in a breath, how dare I keep living it half asleep or chasing other people's definitions of happiness?

It was time to stop surviving by the script and start writing a life that was *my own*.

Excavating the past

In the weeks that followed his funeral, I took long walks around the neighbourhood I grew up in, hoping movement might stir something within me. I thought about my childhood and those elusive years that should have been filled with joy but felt static. I couldn't remember laughter echoing through our home. Only the tense silence between arguments, the shadows that came before bedtime.

It dawned on me that I had spent my entire life mastering dissociation. As a child, I had learned to survive emotional chaos by becoming invisible. Now, as an adult, I was still hiding from others, and from myself.

One afternoon, while rummaging through dusty boxes in storage, I stumbled upon an old photo album. There I was, a child smiling beneath a paper crown, dancing on the roof of my parents' car, running through a field, holding my parents' hands. The images were joyful, but the memories behind them felt inaccessible as if someone had whispered them to me in a dream.

'I can't remember this,' I told my brother, tears slipping down my cheeks.

'It's okay,' he said, his voice gentle. 'Sometimes we block out the things that hurt or maybe you just have a bad memory.'

That night, I began journalling, not for an audience, not for clarity, but simply to connect. I wrote without filters, letting the ink speak truths my voice had never dared. 'What does happiness mean to me?' I scrawled across the top of the page.

The answer didn't come in a revelation, but it came in fragments for me: the scent of jasmine at dusk, the sound of waves crashing on the beach, the quiet satisfaction of doing something kind without anyone watching. Happiness wasn't a destination. It was a return to myself, to simplicity, to stillness.

A new definition

As I peeled back the layers of my life, I began to rebuild, not around perfection but around presence. I stopped saying yes to every invitation. I stopped performing closeness in relationships that no longer felt reciprocal. I made space for solitude, not as punishment, but as sanctuary. I started studying mindset coaching to understand the science behind changing our mindset. And life just got into a rhythm like it always does and you forget about things and get busy with life.

However, there came a point where I knew something had to change and not just on the surface, but at the roots. So, I started over, piece by piece.

I decided to move to a new city, craving for a fresh start in an unfamiliar place where I wasn't defined by history or habit. The move felt symbolic like a physical act of letting go. It wasn't easy, but it was necessary. I was done clinging to the comfort of routines that no longer served me, to friendships that had quietly expired but lingered out of convenience or guilt. It was time to stop apologising for growing in a different direction.

I joined a gym, not to chase an ideal body, but to reconnect with mine. I began attending yoga classes, learning to breathe through discomfort and listen to the signals I had long ignored. In those quiet moments on the mat, something softened. I wasn't trying to prove anything. I was simply trying to be present.

I started agreeing to new adventures instead of reverting to the security of solitude or my comfort zone. I pushed through my social anxiety and started getting involved in community groups and social clubs so I could meet like-minded people, leaving myself open to the potential that strangers might become soul connections. There was something disarming about those interactions. They weren't based on shared pasts or polite obligation; they were rooted in kindness and shared purpose.

I enrolled in an art class, despite the fact I couldn't draw a stick figure to save my life. The goal wasn't mastery. It was joy. It was the freedom of trying, of expressing, of letting go of perfection.

I began travelling alone. No rigid itineraries or curated photo ops, just myself and a willingness to wander. I picked places that made my soul feel wide and alive. Forest trails. Coastal towns. Tiny cafés where no one knew my name. In those moments of quiet exploration, I found something I'd been missing for years: myself.

This wasn't a reinvention. It was recalling, going back to the me that I had buried under expectation, fear and the myth of belonging. And for the first time in a long time, my life didn't feel like a performance. It felt like a conversation with the world, with others and most importantly, with myself.

In time, happiness revealed itself not as a thunderclap, but as a whisper that is consistent, tender and true. It lives in alignment, not applause. In real conversation, not mindless agreement. In the courage to be who you are, even if the world wants a sterilised version.

The harmony of science and spirit

Happiness is not a finish line or destination. Nor is it an accident that befalls the lucky or the perennially sunny. It's a complex, rich phenomenon, and one science has been trying to understand for decades.

Positive psychology, under the leadership of psychologist Martin Seligman, in the late 1990s shifted the focus from mere curing of mental illness to building what a good life looks like. The five pillars on which the PERMA model builds well-being are Positive emotion, Engagement, Relationships, Meaning and Accomplishment. All these, when responsibly developed, lead to a rising and sustainable sense of well-being.

Neuroscience is also crying out for this. Studies have shown that practices like gratitude journalling, meditation and even exercise can actually alter the brain. Concentrating on gratitude, for instance, activates the ventromedial prefrontal cortex, a region in your brain that has been linked with value and reward. With repetition over time, long-term changes to the brain's default programming are possible, shifting attention away from threat and deficit and into appreciation and abundance.

Similarly, Harvard studies have found that mindfulness meditation practised every day not only reduces stress but also leads to an increase in grey matter in areas of the brain associated with memory, empathy and emotional regulation. It's more than a feel-good ritual, it's a neurological reboot.

But science also reminds us that 50% of our happiness is determined by genetics, according to Sonja Lyubomirsky's research. This 'set point' doesn't mean we're doomed to live with whatever temperament we were born with. The remaining is what researchers call intentional activity, is entirely within our control. How we spend our time, how we think, how we relate to others, how we interpret our experiences, these are the levers of happiness we can consciously move.

And let's not forget the social component. Strong social bonds are among the most reliable predictors of long-term happiness. The Harvard Study of Adult Development, where participants have been followed for over 80 years, discovered that good relationships, not money, fame or professional achievement keep individuals healthy and happy. It's not the number of connections, but the quality that is important.

Therefore, happiness is both strongly biological and strongly relational. It is rooted in the body, habituated by repetition and amplified through love, meaning and connection. And yet, there's still a part of happiness that eludes measurement.

Science gives us the structure and the 'how' of happiness.

But the 'why'? That remains beautifully personal. It's found in the hush of a sunrise, the laughter of someone you love, the sacred stillness of feeling aligned with your values. It's the spiritual counterpart to the scientific blueprint. The soul behind the study. So while I turn to science for guidance, I also lean into the mystery. Because some of the happiest moments I've ever had didn't come from a formula. They came from presence. From surrender. From trusting that it's okay not to have all the answers.

Dear reader, this is an invitation for you to begin your own path to happiness.

Happiness isn't something we stumble upon by accident. It's something that we tend with presence, intention and practice. If you've made it this far in this book, perhaps you're already wondering on a deeper level what happiness means for you.

PRACTICAL EXERCISES FOR
NOURISHING YOUR SOUL

1. The 3 good things practice

Time: 5 minutes each evening

Each night before bed, write down three things that went well that day. They don't need to be big and sometimes 'I had a really good coffee' or 'The sunset was beautiful' is enough. This practice, backed by positive psychology research, rewires the brain to notice the good, even in ordinary moments.

Reflection prompt: Why did these moments feel good? What do they reveal about what matters to you?

Notes:

2. Joy mapping

Time: 15–20 minutes, weekly

Draw a circle and mark it with things, people, places or activities that make you feel really alive, peaceful or happy. This is your 'joy map'. Build upon it over time. Let it evolve. Then, choose one thing per week to deliberately schedule into your calendar.

Reflection prompt: What do you notice? Are there sources of joy that you've been underutilising?

3. Values check-in

Time: 30 minutes (monthly review recommended)

List your top 5 personal values (e.g. autonomy, belonging, freedom, imagination, honesty, rest). Then, ask yourself: Am I living in alignment with these values? Where am I living them out? Where am I selling out?

Reflection prompt: What small shifts can I make this week to live more fully in alignment?

4. Authenticity audit

Time: As needed, especially following social interactions

Take a break after a social interaction or conversation and check in with yourself.

Reflection prompt: Ask yourself ...

- Did I feel seen?
- Was I myself?
- Did I love that connection and feel energised, or did it leave me drained out?

Action step: Begin saying 'yes' to environments that energise you and 'no' to those that require a show.

5. Presence ritual

Time: 1–10 minutes a day

Choose a simple everyday habit that keeps you present e.g., a distraction-free cup of tea, a slow stroll around the block, 10 mindful breaths at your desk. Make it your anchor.

Set the intention: Happiness is in the here and now, not the tomorrow.

Practise it daily for at least 1 week and see how you feel.

Notes:

ON A FINAL NOTE

This is your invitation to look inside. To ask the hard questions. To listen for the quiet answers. And to remember happiness is not a destination you arrive at. It's a rhythm you learn to dance to.

One intentional step at a time.

You don't need to overhaul your life to be happy. You just need to start where you are with curiosity, with courage and with kindness to yourself.

PART 2

CULTIVATING INNER HAPPINESS

CHAPTER 3

Rediscovering yourself: the art of coming home to yourself

ON A RANDOM Sunday while standing alone in front of my closet, the doors slammed open like an epiphany. Shirts hung limply over racks. Dresses, once worn with purpose, sagged in silence. The shoes at the bottom with the heels I wore to corporate presentations, the sneakers from weekend brunches and the sandals from romantic getaways, all just sat there in judgemental stillness. Each item represented a version of me I had carefully constructed over the years… the high-achieving employee, the ever-available and understanding friend, the partner who always put others first. And yet, in that moment, every piece felt alien. It was as if I had raided a stranger's closet.

There is something deeply disorienting about waking up one day and realising that the life you're living no longer feels like your own. No catastrophic event had triggered it. No big breakup, no job loss, no dramatic fallout. Instead, it was a slow erosion, a silent unravelling so gradual that I hadn't noticed how much of myself I'd lost until the absence became unbearable.

When burnout wears your name

Burnout doesn't always roar. Sometimes it arrives quietly, like fog seeping through the cracks. Mine crept in through endless to-do lists and late-night emails, camouflaged as ambition. I convinced myself that being busy meant being valuable. I used to pride myself on how much I could juggle. I would call myself *"The Queen of Multitasking"*. But beneath the surface, something was breaking.

Weekdays bled into weekends. Mornings began with a screech and ended with exhaustion. My life had become a series of transactional deliverables, deadlines and decisions. I stopped doing things that weren't 'productive'. I stopped reading fictional novels like I used to. I stopped doing my morning yoga routine. I even stopped taking long showers, replacing them with speed washes to save time for more work.

The final straw wasn't dramatic. It came on an ordinary Thursday afternoon, during a routine catch-up at work.

'You've been quiet lately,' a colleague said gently, looking at me with curiosity more than concern.

'Just busy,' I replied with the kind of smile that looks convincing on the outside and feels hollow on the inside.

That evening, I sat alone in my apartment, scrolling through a social media feed filled with people seemingly thriving. Friends hiking through forests, swimming in oceans, laughing at candlelit dinners. I had the same social media profile too, but I didn't really feel it was real. I felt like I was observing life through glass, distanced not just by geography but by spirit. The contrast between the joy in my social media photos and my numbness in real life hit me with a kind of violence.

This isn't living, I thought. Not with despair, but with clarity.

The forgotten pages

And then something unexpected happened. Whenever I am stressed, I initiate a big clean-up to clean the clutter out of my life, and that's what I started doing. While sorting through paperwork in a drawer I hadn't opened in years, I found an old journal. The cover was worn, the pages ink-stained and dog-eared. I opened it and was immediately transported back to a time when I wrote just for the joy of it about what I wanted from my future life. Page after page was filled with musings, poetry, goals, doodles, raw and unedited pieces of me that had once burned brightly. Quotes I had once believed in. Lines like:

'One day I'll write a book.'

'I want to dance under a foreign sky.'

'My life will be big and soft and full of art & music.'

One entry stood out. Dated six years ago, it ended with a simple reminder: *Remember who you are.* This was something I wrote as I was just going through the separation with my ex-husband, a big turning point in my life.

I wept not from sadness, but from recognition.

That was the moment I knew something had to change. Not a surface-level fix like a new skincare routine or a vacation escape. What I needed was a complete reorientation. I had to rediscover myself, not the polished LinkedIn version but the unfiltered human underneath the layers of performance.

I started small.

First, I did what I now call an 'identity inventory'. I sat down with a notebook and listed every role I'd played in recent years: professional, partner, friend, daughter, achiever. For each role, I asked two questions:

Does this still serve me? and *Do I feel seen or valued in this role or just useful?*

The answers were sobering. I realised how often I'd made decisions to be liked, to avoid conflict or to meet someone else's expectations. In doing so, I'd become hyper competent but emotionally malnourished. I wasn't living *my* life. I was curating a version of it for the comfort of others.

So I went deeper. I created what I called a *values map*: a handwritten chart of the things that truly mattered to me, independent of anyone's opinion. Creativity. Connection. Freedom. Integrity. Stillness. These weren't just words. They were north stars I had long neglected.

Next came the rituals

I began taking long walks without my phone, just to be present. I started journalling again without judgement, without audience, without purpose other than to hear myself think. I sat at the beach with my dog and people watched. I started re-reading books that once inspired me. I let silence fill my space without rushing to mute it with noise. I started enjoying my company again, not trying to fill every space with something to do.

I also took more courageous steps. I said no to social events that felt performative. I set boundaries at work, declining after-hours requests that compromised my well-being. I let go of relationships that only thrived when I over-gave. I realised some of my friendships only existed because I made myself available based on others needs but it was never reciprocated.

The truth about rediscovery is that it isn't always fun or romantic. Sometimes it feels like grief. You mourn the version of yourself that worked so hard to belong. You grieve the time lost in becoming someone others approved of. But in that shedding, you also find liberation.

In time, I began to feel the return of something precious, 'feeling like myself'. Feeling alive. It arrived in flickers: laughter that wasn't forced, curiosity that wasn't performative, moments of stillness that felt sacred. I felt like I was reclaiming space within my own body, stepping out of a performance and into presence.

I followed joy like breadcrumbs.

One weekend, I booked a solo trip to the coast, walking along the cliffs with the wind in my hair and the smell of salt in the air. Another weekend, I took a pottery class; my bowl was lopsided, but I hadn't felt so creatively free in years. I began dancing in my kitchen again, barefoot, wine glass in hand, music on full blast.

And slowly, I noticed something else: the more I aligned with who I really was, the less I needed external validation. I didn't need applause. I didn't crave constant praise. I was living in harmony with my truth and that, it turned out, was more satisfying than anything I'd previously pursued.

I don't have a dramatic ending for you. There was no fireworks moment, no viral transformation, no grand revelation that made everything better. What I have instead is something quieter and more lasting.

I have peace.

I have clarity.

I have myself.

If you're reading this and feel like a stranger in your own life, know that you're not alone. You haven't failed. You're just overdue for a reunion with your own soul.

Start where you are. Start messy. Start with a walk. Start

with a journal. Start by asking, *What lights me up?* Then follow the answer even if it's only a flicker. Trust it.

Because rediscovery is not about reinventing who you are. It's about peeling away what you're not.

It's about coming home.

And you, my friend, deserve to be home in your own life.

PRACTICAL EXERCISES TO
FIND YOURSELF AGAIN

These exercises are designed to help your process of rediscovering who you are beyond roles, expectations and habits. Use them as a tool to reconnect with yourself, clarify your values and create space for what matters most.

1. Identity inventory

Purpose: To reflect on the roles you've played in life and evaluate which ones still serve your true self.

e.g. Roles I've played: manager, wife, best friend.

List all the roles you've played in the last 5 to 10 years, both professional and personal. Then reflect on each using these prompts:

Role	Why did I take on this role?	Do I still resonate with it?	Do I feel seen in this role, or just useful?	Keep / release / redefine

Role	Why did I take on this role?	Do I still resonate with it?	Do I feel seen in this role, or just useful?	Keep / release / redefine

2. Core values discovery map

Purpose: To find the personal values that guide your most satisfying decisions and relationships.

Start writing down the core values that resonate with you. Then choose your top 5 core values by circling them and write how each one is (or isn't) being expressed in your life right now.

E.g. My top 5 core values are: creativity, connection, peace, freedom and nature.

Core value	Why does this matter to me?	Am I living it fully today?	What would honouring this value look like?

Core value	Why does this matter to me?	Am I living it fully today?	What would honouring this value look like?

3. Joy breadcrumb tracker

Purpose: To help you notice small, ordinary sparks of joy and build a life with more of them.

For a week, write down moments of joy, calm, awe or inspiration. It could be as simple as drinking a cup of coffee in the morning alone, or a good night kiss from your child.

Date	Joyful moment	What did it feel like?	How can I create more of this?

Date	Joyful moment	What did it feel like?	How can I create more of this?
		53	

Date	Joyful moment	What did it feel like?	How can I create more of this?

4. Rediscovery roadmap

Purpose: To craft a personal plan for reconnecting with yourself and making conscious life changes.

Answer each section truthfully. Let this be your guide.

1. What I want more of in my life:

2. What I want less of in my life:

3. What makes me feel most like myself:

____

4. One small change I can make this week:

____

5. One brave decision I want to make this month:

____

ON A FINAL NOTE

Rediscovering yourself is not a destination. It's a journey. A choice. A commitment to look within when the world demands that you look outside.

I still work today. I still show up for others. But no longer do I abandon myself in that process.

I'm bolder now and softer too. I know that I cannot be measured by a title or a list of tasks done well.

I know who I am at my core through this process of rediscovering myself. And I am free.

CHAPTER 4

Changing your mindset, changing your life

For as long as I can remember, a quiet but powerful belief has shadowed me: *I'm not good enough*.

It didn't shout. It didn't need to. It whispered in moments of hesitation, echoed in periods of silence, and took root in the pauses between accomplishment and recognition. This belief, this unspoken burden, shaped the way I expressed myself to the world. In job interviews, I questioned every word. With friends, I did not want to let my guard down. In moments of triumph, I downplayed my accomplishments. It was not humility. It was self-doubt masquerading as humility.

The epiphany came during what was, quite literally, a regular performance review. I sat facing my manager, a poised and highly respected woman whom I greatly admired. She read out my achievements in measured tones, pausing occasionally to offer thoughtful compliments. But while she listed my achievements, I was cataloguing my failures.

She stopped mid-sentence and looked me in the eye. 'You have a lot of potential, Charu. But you have to believe in yourself.'

Her words struck me with startling clarity. It wasn't criticism. It was concern. I walked out of that room feeling raw and exposed. Later that night, I sat in front of the mirror and asked myself a question I had long avoided: *Why do I think I'm not enough?*

It wasn't easy to face. It was easier to push through with productivity, to hide beneath the to-do lists, perfectionism and the need for approval. But that night, something changed. I was done running.

The work of undoing beliefs

Self-transformation isn't just an Instagram quote or a weekend retreat. It's a messy, lonely and often painful process of unlearning and relearning. For months, I looked inward and asked myself the same hard questions every night:

- What stories do I believe about myself?
- Where did they come from?
- Who taught me that I needed to earn worthiness?

And maybe most importantly: *Are these stories true?*

Most weren't. Some were echoes of a perfectionist childhood. Others were shaped by a culture that values output over humanity. A few were formed through failure, misinterpreted as permanent truths instead of temporary lessons.

The belief that I wasn't enough was not formed in a single moment. It was cultivated over many years. And undoing it meant facing each moment it had been reinforced and consciously rewriting the script.

At a dinner party, someone casually asked about my ambitions as a mindset coach. 'I don't know,' I said. 'I feel like it's too late to start now. And with my schedule, I just don't have the time.' It was a well-rehearsed answer. Polite. Justified. And untrue.

My friend looked at me, genuinely confused. 'Too late? Charu, what are you talking about? You're just getting started.'

It wasn't a pep talk. It wasn't even particularly profound. But the simplicity of her disbelief cracked something open in me. Her words didn't just challenge my statement. They challenged the foundation it stood on.

Thought work and healing

This was one of those moments when something shifted in me again, and I made a commitment to myself to live more intentionally moving forward not just to challenge my thoughts but to actively change them. I borrowed tools from cognitive behavioural therapy (CBT), neuroscience and spiritual practices. I read multiple books on techniques that could help people, and with my education in mindset coaching, I had a solid background on where to start. Some examples of practices that helped me the most are described below.

Cognitive reframing

When my mind whispered, 'You can't do this,' I replaced it with, 'You are learning.'

'What if I fail?' became, 'What if I grow through this?'

Instead of internalising every misstep as a character flaw, I reframed them as stepping stones. Setbacks became feedback.

Visualisation and embodiment

Each morning, before I checked my phone or opened my laptop, I sat in stillness and visualised my future self as confident, grounded and leading workshops while connecting with others. I didn't just see her. I felt her energy. I breathed as she did. I walked differently because of it.

Affirmations rooted in truth

Rather than forcing toxic positivity, I created affirmations that felt authentic:

- 'I am in the process of building confidence.'
- 'I trust myself more each day.'
- 'I have permission to succeed in my own way.'

Over time, these statements formed a bridge between who I had been and who I was becoming.

Compassionate self-inquiry

Healing requires understanding, so I became curious about my inner critic. I began to recognise its tone, its origin and its intentions. Often, it was trying to protect me from embarrassment or disappointment. But its methods were outdated.

Instead of silencing the voice, I started speaking to it: 'I know you're trying to keep me safe, but I don't need that kind of protection anymore.'

Building a new inner world

Eventually, I began to notice a change. Subtle at first. I spoke up in meetings. I stopped over-apologising. I pitched a coaching program at work. I said no without guilt. I took up space without shame. I started pushing back on one-sided friendships that I was maintaining just for the sake of holding on to old friends. I started writing about my life, ideas and thoughts every day, which eventually led me in the direction of writing this book.

And when the voice of 'not good enough' returned because it always tries to come back, I met it with new wisdom:

'Thank you for your concern, but I'm doing things differently now.'

However, this journey isn't a straight line. Some days I still falter. I question myself. I fear I'm not doing enough. But I no longer believe that fear is evidence that I can't. I now understand it's a sign that I'm expanding & growing.

If you're on the edge of your own shift, here is what I want you to know:

- You are not broken or less than anyone else.
- Your mindset does not have to be fixed in the same state forever.
- The stories you inherited are not your destiny.

Change is not reserved for the privileged, the extroverted or the endlessly confident. It is available to all of us, in the quiet moments we choose courage over comfort.

You may not silence every doubt. But you can speak louder than it.

PRACTICAL EXERCISES FOR MINDSET JOURNALLING

Use the below exercises to begin shifting your story. Repeat this as often as needed. Mindset isn't a destination; it's a daily practice.

1. Mindset shift practice

Use this guided worksheet to help you identify, challenge and reframe limiting beliefs that may be holding you back.

Identifying limiting beliefs

What belief is holding you back right now?

When did you first start believing this?

Who or what influenced this belief?

Challenging the belief

What evidence supports this belief?

What evidence contradicts this belief?

How has this belief impacted your life negatively?

Reframing the belief

What would a more empowering belief be?

How would this new belief change the way you act or feel?

Write a personal affirmation based on this new belief:

Daily practice

List 3 affirmations you will repeat daily:

What is one action you will take today aligned with your new belief?

____

____

____

Your story isn't finished

ON A FINAL NOTE

My journey of rewriting my mindset has become the most liberating work of my life. It didn't require external permission, massive wealth or perfect timing. It required presence. Honesty. And a relentless willingness to return to the truth.

You are not the voice of your doubt. You are the author of your future.

So take the pen. Write differently. Believe deeper. And above all, live as if you already are who you're becoming.

Because you are.

CHAPTER 5

Habit forming and the power of micro changes

BEFORE I UNDERSTOOD the true nature of change, my life was a constant performance. I woke up every morning and put on the same invisible suit of the high-functioning professional, the good friend, the well-put-together woman who made it all look effortless. It was like Groundhog Day every day. Wake up, scroll phone, work, repeat. I wasn't miserable, but I wasn't alive either. I was existing on autopilot repeating habits and patterns that no longer served me but felt too ingrained to question.

The weight of it came to a head on an unremarkable Monday night, which turned out to be another moment of awakening for me. I made myself a cup of peppermint tea before bed, more out of routine than comfort, and stepped out onto my tiny apartment balcony. It was quiet, the sort of quiet that makes you notice everything like the hum of the city in the distance, the rustle of leaves in the wind, the heaviness in your own body. I looked up at the sky and noticed the stars, *really* noticed them, perhaps for the first time in months. And amidst that silence, a question arose, not loud but clear: *What if the answer isn't more but less, just more thoughtfully?*

The myth of the big change

In a culture obsessed with reinvention, we have a tendency to mythologise change as something seismic. We crave before and after moments of drama of the overnight successes, complete makeovers, comprehensive resolutions, that will have us cured by Monday. But real change, I would soon learn, rarely, if ever, arrives in tidal waves. It arrives as ripples, small and incremental movements that shift our inner landscape by degrees.

The next morning, I did something small. So small it felt almost ridiculous. I opened an old notebook and gave myself five minutes to write with no rules, no pressure, just whatever surfaced. I don't remember what I wrote that day. It might have been mundane. It might have been hopeful. But what I do remember is the sensation. For the first time in a long while, I felt as though I had taken one small step back towards myself.

That five-minute journalling ritual became my first micro habit. I didn't call it that at the time. I wasn't trying to overhaul my life or fix anything. I just knew that those five minutes grounded me. They gave me something to return to… a thread of intention in a day otherwise ruled by noise.

As days passed, I noticed a ripple effect. Writing down my thoughts cleared space in my mind. I became more articulate in meetings. My ideas felt sharper. I started responding rather than reacting. Then, without meaning to, I added another tiny ritual. Each morning, before my coffee, I drank a glass of water. It seems silly, even now, to call that a habit. But it shifted something within me. It was a decision, a declaration that my well-being mattered and that my body deserved care before caffeine. Soon, my morning walks extended from 10 minutes to 30 minutes. I began listening to music I loved again. I left my phone behind sometimes just to breathe in and be present in nature.

None of these changes were dramatic. If you had looked at my life from the outside, you might not have noticed anything different. But inside, I was undergoing a quiet revolution. For the first time in years, I was making decisions that didn't come from fear or pressure or obligation, they came from self-respect.

The science of micro habits

It turns out there's science behind this. Our brains are wired to resist overwhelming change. When we try to radically shift our routines, set enormous goals or declare sweeping resolutions, our nervous system often registers this as a threat. That's why so many diets, routines and New Year's resolutions unravel by February. But micro habits, which are tiny, repeatable actions that require minimal effort, bypass that resistance. They sneak past the alarm system. And over time, they change everything.

According to neuroscience, small, repeated behaviours rewire the brain through neuroplasticity, strengthening the neural pathways employed in the habits we execute most frequently. It is not the size of the change that matters, as author James Clear illustrates in *Atomic Habits*, but the consistency with which you implement it. Small habits, accumulated day by day, snowball into impactful change.

The more I leaned into micro habits, the more I realised their power to dismantle long-held beliefs. I began questioning the voice in my head that told me I had to earn rest. That I needed to accomplish something big to be worthy of happiness. That I wasn't doing enough. I replaced those thoughts with new ones, one small action at a time. I wasn't trying to become someone else. I was remembering who I truly was beneath the noise, the roles and the performance.

The brilliance of micro habits lies in their resistance to overwhelm. When we aim to 'overhaul' our lives, we trigger fear, resistance and perfectionism. But brushing your teeth and whispering one thing you're grateful for? That's achievable. That's sustainable.

Behavioural psychologist BJ Fogg, founder of Stanford's Behaviour Design Lab, calls this the 'anchor method'. By tying a new habit to an existing one, such as taking three deep breaths after pouring your morning coffee, you reduce the mental friction of starting. The cue is built in. The reward is internal and the change becomes automatic.

The benefit I was most surprised at was how kind this approach felt. There was no room for perfectionism. If I missed a day, I didn't spiral into guilt. I just picked it up the next day. There was no failure, only a gentle return. I stopped measuring progress based on outcome and started measuring it by alignment. Did this practice bring me closer to who I was becoming? Did it taste of kindness? And if so, it counted.

One of the most significant shifts I made was in the way I set my goals. Instead of saying, 'I want to be more productive,' I began saying, *'I'm someone who honours their time.'* Instead of 'I want to lose weight,' it became, *'I'm becoming someone who cares for their body with love.'* This subtle shift from outcome driven goals to identity-based intentions helped me embody the very habits I wanted to cultivate.

It wasn't about fixing myself. It was about becoming more me.

Now, when people ask me how I found happiness, I don't mention a single event or a dramatic breakthrough. I talk about small things. The five minutes of journalling. The morning sunlight on my skin. The phone-free walks on the beach. The ability I developed to hold myself back and breathe before responding to someone's criticism. The sticky notes on my mirror reminding me to drink water. The song I play when I need to shift my energy. These things may seem trivial. But strung together, they formed the thread that stitched me back to myself.

A pathway for change. Start small, start today

If you're feeling stuck, like I was, you don't need a 90-day plan or a 5 am wake-up call. You need one, small, self-honouring act. Here's how to begin:

- **Choose one micro habit – so small it seems almost insignificant**: One push-up. One line written in your journal. One minute of breathing. One glass of water as you wake up.
- **Anchor it to something you already do**: 'After I brush my teeth, I will…' This makes it habitual.
- **Have a visual tracker:** A notebook, calendar or habit tracker will suffice. Visual reinforcement builds momentum.
- **Celebrate right away:** Fist pump. Smile. Whisper, 'Yes.' Celebrate as if it counts, because it does.
- **Be gentle with setbacks**: Consistency is more important than perfection. Getting a day behind isn't failure. Quitting is. Just begin again tomorrow.

And most importantly, give yourself grace. You are not behind. You are not broken. You are human, and you are already capable of more than you know.

PRACTICAL EXERCISES TO CHANGE YOUR HABITS

1. The 7-Day Micro Habit Challenge

If you're ready to experiment, I invite you to take the 7-Day Micro Habit Challenge. Choose one small act aligned with an area of your life that feels heavy. Commit to it daily for a week. Track your reflections using the tracker below. Celebrate your wins.

By the end of the week, you may not have a new life but you'll have a new rhythm. And from rhythm comes momentum. From momentum, transformation.

This printable toolkit is designed to help you begin your micro habit journey. Use this space to track your daily progress, reflect on your experiences and build habits that reconnect you with your authentic self. Remember: small steps, taken consistently, create lasting transformation.

Micro habit tracker

Day	Micro habit completed? (Y/N)	Reflection / How did it feel?
Day 1		
Day 2		
Day 3		
Day 4		
Day 5		
Day 6		
Day 7		

Micro habit journalling prompts

What small habit made the biggest difference in your day?

When did you feel most connected to yourself this week?

How did you respond to moments of resistance or challenge?

What would you like to carry forward from this experience?

Describe a moment you felt proud of yourself this week.

What is one habit you would like to build next, and why?

ON A FINAL NOTE

Change isn't always loud. Sometimes it whispers. Sometimes it begins with a teacup, a quiet balcony and a notebook waiting to catch your thoughts. And sometimes it begins with a decision so small it barely registers until one day, you look up and realise you've rewritten your life, one micro moment at a time.

Happiness, I've come to understand, is not found in far-off destinations or in future versions of ourselves. It's in the mundane, the present and the choices we make when no one is watching. It's in the way we talk to ourselves when we wake up and when we fail. It's not the mountain climbed; it's the step taken, again and again.

Start small. Dream big. And trust that the gentle power of micro change is more than enough.

CHAPTER 6

Gratitude and the power of daily appreciation

In a world that's increasingly measured by what we do, what we have and what we endure, gratitude can be a luxury like a soft whisper in a society that's only going to listen to screams. But for me, it was a lifeline.

There was no moment of great epiphany, no turning point, just a quiet afternoon, the dull hum of city noise outside, and a kind of aching stillness that had settled in my bones. It was when the Covid-19 lockdowns had just started in 2020 that the walls of my small apartment felt like they were closing in. The silence echoed my loneliness, and I often found myself spiralling into despair. I was still functioning, still ticking boxes, showing up for work calls, answering emails but internally, I felt like I was slowly eroding.

It was during one of these foggy, heavy days that I reached for my notebook. Not because I knew what to do, but because I didn't. Something within me, a whisper I could barely hear, suggested a simple action: *Write down three things you're grateful for.*

I was initially reluctant. It felt cliché. How would a list of good things change the crushing weight I was feeling? But I did it anyway perhaps out of desperation, or faint hope.

1. *The smell of fresh coffee*
2. *A warm cup of tea*
3. *Laughter shared with friends*

That was it. Just three small things. But in the stillness that followed, something inside me softened.

That first entry wasn't poetic or profound. But it was real. I paused after each item, letting it sink in. The rich aroma of freshly brewed coffee in the morning wrapped around me like a warm hug, ushering me into the day ahead. The tea at night was a ritual for me, a moment to inhale deeply, savour heat between my hands and come to life in the middle of chaos. And I could hear my friend Kat bursting into laughter on the phone with me following suit after some random comment we both found hilarious; the kind of laughter that erupts from deep within, impossible to ignore, cutting through the monotony of a long week.

'Can it really be this simple?' I wondered aloud as I tucked the notebook away. But something inside shifted; gratitude breathed life into ordinary moments that had previously passed unnoticed.

It was the beginning of a slow shift. I wasn't suddenly healed or transformed. But I had started to plant a few seeds.

Day after day, weeks passed and this small habit grew from duty to delight. Each morning before diving into office or house work, I wrote down three things that had brought light to my world. With time, the practice of recording gratitude became ritual.

Some days, the entries came easily like a stunning sunset, an overdue message from a friend, the comfort of my dog curling up beside me. Other days, I had to dig deeper: 'The ability to cry,' I wrote once. 'The fact that I'm alive' I wrote while listening to Covid death tolls on the news.

But even on those harder days, the practice grounded me. I wasn't denying the difficult aspects; I was choosing to honour what was good alongside it.

What surprised me most was how my life began to change. My thoughts once so easily pulled towards what was missing or broken now had an anchor. Gratitude didn't erase pain or difficulty, but it simply offered me a different way to carry it. Instead of contemplating challenges or setbacks, I began to appreciate the hidden gifts nestled within those experiences.

'Your contract at work is coming to an end?' A friend said one evening over pizza. 'Think of it as a chance to grow!'

Her words hit home harder than any motivational speech ever could. In that moment, losing my job transformed from shattering news into an instant possibility for pursuing new dreams and greater opportunities, with the world nudging me towards untapped potential rather than closing doors.

Eventually, I began to weave reminders into my space. A rock on my desk with 'Breathe' carved into it. A post-it note on my mirror reading, 'Today, find something beautiful.' These small visual cues helped ground me in the present and remind me that I had more power than I realised. I bought this cute deck of cards with little motivational messages on them. I kept it at my desk, and every morning I would take out a new card, which I considered my personal memo from the universe for the day. It was the most amazing thing to read 'Believe' or 'Take a risk' and it was a genuinely fun way of changing my mindset that has stuck with me.

Every now and then, I'd stumble upon photographs tucked away in drawers, snapshots that captured laughter shared under sunlit skies or candid moments where love overflowed in friendships. These pictures reminded me of those joyful times when life felt limitless and showed me that there can be beauty in just a few seconds, rather than in grand gestures.

Perhaps the most powerful shift was that I began to write gratitude letters, less for the purpose of sending them and more for the purpose of releasing what had lingered unsaid. I wrote one to my mum. It wasn't polished or perfect. It was raw and honest, brimming with appreciation for the sacrifices she had made and the strength she modelled, often silently. Tears fell freely as I wrote, each one softening a part of me I didn't know had hardened.

As a child, expressions of affection were not a part of my home. Love was acted out, in duties fulfilled but rarely spoken. As an adult, I deliberately rewrote that script in my relationships. I tell my partner I love him every day. I send silly 'miss you' messages and pictures to my brother. I hug my friends tightly and tell them exactly why I appreciate them.

But with my mother, I had to accept that some relationships exist outside that kind of exchange. And that's okay. That letter was never meant for her to read; it was meant for me. Because here's the truth… gratitude is not about performance. It's about presence. It doesn't need an audience. It needs intention.

Another great tool, introduced to me by a friend, was breathwork. When I first heard about it, I was reluctant, but I agreed to give it a try. I didn't do anything fancy, just simple breathing with a mindful inhale and exhale. Pairing gratitude with breathwork added a new dimension. With each deep inhale, I invited calm. With each exhale, I released tension. On the days when my mind was cloudy or my nerves were frayed, returning to my breath anchored by gratitude restored a sense of control. It was like telling my nervous system, 'You are safe. There is still good here.'

This somatic practice brought a bodily appreciation of gratitude that writing alone could not. The breath was a bridge between thinking and feeling, between acknowledging joy in the mind and sensing it in the body.

Gratitude is not about pretending. It's about perspective.

There's a common misconception that gratitude is a way of denying pain. That being grateful means you have to ignore what's hard. But it's quite the opposite. Gratitude is a lens, not a blindfold. It says, *This is difficult… and still, there is light.*

Even during periods of job instability, personal heartbreak, uncertainty in life, I found myself a little more resilient, a little more attuned to what was working. Gratitude became my counterweight to despair. It gave me the courage to keep showing up, to keep hoping, to keep trying.

It was not a cure. It was a compass.

PRACTICAL EXERCISES FOR
DAILY APPRECIATION

Here is an invitation for you. If you're reading this and feeling like life is too heavy, too complicated, too far gone, start here:

Each day, write down three things you're grateful for.

They don't have to be profound. They don't even have to make sense to anyone else. Just make them yours. A smell. A texture. A memory. A moment of silence. A person who stayed.

And when the world feels like it's closing in, when everything feels uncertain, come back to that list. Let it remind you that beauty, however fleeting, is still part of your story.

Because gratitude isn't about what you have. It's about how you see what you have.

And once you start to see clearly, everything changes.

Here is a space for you to start this process with a template for the next five days. You can start the process here and then continue in your journal.

Hold onto simple joys in life, because eventually you'll realise they were the milestones that mattered most.

Day 1: Today I'm grateful for:

Gratitude #1	
Gratitude #2	
Gratitude #3	
Reflection notes	

Day 2: Today I'm grateful for:

Gratitude #1	
Gratitude #2	
Gratitude #3	
Reflection notes	

Day 3: Today I'm grateful for:

Gratitude #1	
Gratitude #2	
Gratitude #3	
Reflection notes	

Day 4: Today I'm grateful for:

Gratitude #1	
Gratitude #2	
Gratitude #3	
Reflection notes	

Day 5: Today I'm grateful for:

Gratitude #1	
Gratitude #2	
Gratitude #3	
Reflection notes	

ON A FINAL NOTE

In the quiet moments when life feels overwhelming this practice offers a gentle reminder that beauty exists all around you even in the smallest things; all you have to do is see them as they are. You don't need a big reason to be thankful to the universe. You only need a small moment of joy, a breath to show you are living and breathing, and a willingness to see the world with softer eyes.

So keep a pen handy. Keep noticing. Keep returning to the goodness around you, again and again. Because even on the hardest days there will always be something worth appreciating, no matter how small, and often this is where healing begins and joy follows.

PART 3

HAPPINESS IN RELATIONSHIPS

CHAPTER 7

Healing the past with forgiveness and letting go

AFTER MY DIVORCE, the echoes of my marriage still lingered like shadows around me wherever I went. There were days I thought I had moved on and that the weight had lifted. But then a smell, a sound, a photograph brought it all rushing back, not the good memories, but the questions, the confusion, the grief of a love that twisted itself into something very unrecognisable to me.

When we first met, I was 18 years old and fresh out of school in Delhi, young and full of dreams. I truly believed I had found the kind of love I had always hoped for. He was charming, warm and emotionally aware, or so I thought. He said all the right things. He told me he never wanted to be like the men he had grown up around. I saw that as a sign of growth and self-awareness. I believed him. I built a future with him. I silenced my parents' warnings. I ignored the discomfort I felt when I caught glimpses of a different side of him during our fights. I called it stress, or culture clash, or temporary friction. I was in love, and I was committed. That meant making things work through good times and bad.

But the man I married wasn't the same man I stayed married to. There's a specific kind of heartbreak that comes from loving someone who slowly becomes a different person. It's not like a breakup where things fall apart quickly, loudly, visibly. This was different. This was a slow fade, a disintegration so subtle that by the time I realised what I had become, I could barely remember who I was.

He changed or maybe he revealed who he had always been, but I was too naïve or too in love to see it. The warmth turned cold. The apologies stopped coming. And in their place grew a greed for control, accusations and silence. I started feeling like I lived in a house where my voice didn't matter. Where my needs were dismissed. Where I was expected to give endlessly and receive nothing in return. I found myself constantly adjusting to his moods, walking on thin ice, shrinking myself to avoid conflict, questioning my own reality. I began to lose my grip on the timeline of things, and sometimes I would ask myself, *'Was it always this way? Am I overreacting? Maybe if I just give a little more and try a little harder, he'll become the man I remember…'*

There were nights when I cried myself to sleep, wondering what I had done wrong. I kept telling myself this wasn't abuse. After all, he wasn't hitting me. But the truth is, emotional abuse is more subtle. It seeps into your self-esteem, slowly rewiring your thoughts until you no longer believe in your own version of the story. It convinces you that your worth is conditional and that love must be earned through sacrifice. I kept telling myself that marriage is hard and love is about compromise, that I had made a commitment and I was willing to uphold that commitment at any cost… until the cost was almost my life.

One rainy afternoon, I sat on the edge of my bed, holding

a photograph from what felt like another lifetime. Our smiles beamed at the camera, the kind of smile that hides everything beneath it. Looking at that image, I didn't see any joy. I saw denial. I saw a woman trying desperately to believe in something that was already gone. I saw a version of myself who had loved blindly, completely and without reserve and who had been left in pieces.

The breaking point wasn't a dramatic fight or a final betrayal. It was the moment I realised I was no longer part of a marriage, but a transaction negotiated not between two people who had once loved each other, but between me and his parents, with him standing silently on their side.

After a particularly painful fallout with him, when I had returned from visiting my parents, hoping for a reset and that maybe some space would soften what had become of us, he sat me down with a chilling calm. There was no apology. No acknowledgment of the chaos or pain we had endured. Instead, he presented me with a set of conditions his parents had drawn up: a manifesto of how I should live if I wanted to remain in their son's life.

And when I looked at him, hoping for some sign of hesitation or a flicker of the man I once loved, all I saw was certainty. He believed this was reasonable. He believed this was how things ought to be.

I remember laughing not because it was funny, but because I was in disbelief. I had spent years fighting for our relationship, defending it when others questioned it and giving him the benefit of every doubt. And now, here he was, standing firmly behind a list that stripped me of my identity, independence and dignity.

That moment broke something in me. It wasn't loud. It

didn't come with shouting or slamming doors. It was quiet, final and hollow like the sound of something precious cracking on the inside. That was the moment I stopped trying. The moment I knew I couldn't save us. The moment I realised I wasn't being loved; I was being controlled.

That moment was the beginning of the end and, though I didn't know it yet, the beginning of me finding my way back to myself.

The turning point for me

It wasn't a dramatic moment that changed everything. It was a quiet, almost invisible shift during a coaching session. My mindset coach, with soft steadiness, asked me the question that would change my life:

'What do you need to let go of?'

I felt the words crack something open in me. The tears came hard and fast, not just for him but for *me*. For the woman I had abandoned in the process of trying to keep a marriage alive. For the version of me that accepted pain and called it compromise. For the girl who once believed that love was supposed to hurt a little.

Because the hardest part wasn't just the pain, it was the confusion. The man I loved in the beginning wasn't the man I ended up with. He shifted slowly, and then all at once. He started with the soft apologies, the tenderness and the promises. But somewhere along the way, he became someone I didn't recognise. Someone colder. Crueller. Someone who saw my love not as something to cherish but to control.

That's the particular kind of trauma no one warns you about… the grief of losing someone who is still alive, still in front of you, but no longer the person you once knew. I stayed far longer than I should have not because I didn't see the truth, but because I was grieving the ghost of the man I fell in love with, while trying to survive the one I was married to.

That night, I sat down and wrote a letter to him. Not for him to read, but for me to release.

'Dear [his name],

I forgive you not because you deserve it, but because I deserve peace.'

.....

The words flowed out like they had been waiting for my permission. I wrote about the confusion, the manipulation, the coldness that replaced connection. I wrote about the girl I used to be, the one who believed in love, who believed in him. I didn't excuse his actions. I didn't minimise the pain. But I let the story leave my body and live on the page.

When I finished, I cried a lot. Not the kind of crying that leaves you empty, but the kind that releases and creates space. I folded the letter and slipped it into my journal. It wasn't a grand gesture, but it felt like the beginning of something. A soft exhale after years of holding my breath.

Understanding forgiveness

Forgiveness didn't come all at once. It wasn't a noble act of closure or an instantaneous feeling of freedom. It came in fragments. In moments when I chose to stop replaying conversations in my mind. In moments when I stopped checking his social media. In moments when I could talk about what happened without shaking or ending up in tears.

It was less about him and more about me. About reclaiming the parts of myself that I had given up in the name of survival.

I started creating small rituals around release. One night when I was feeling a little under the weather, I wrote down every resentment I had on a piece of paper, and then burned it. I watched the corners of it curl into ash and drift away. And with it, something inside me loosened. The bitterness I had clung to like armour no longer felt necessary. I didn't need to hate him to prove that he had hurt me. I didn't need to hold on to the pain to validate my story.

What I learned from this process of healing and letting go is that forgiveness is not a transaction. It's not earned. It's not even about the other person. True forgiveness is the slow, patient act of uncaging your spirit from a memory that no longer serves you.

It's the decision to stop bleeding for someone who never brought you a bandage.

And it unfolds in layers, like the petals of a flower in sunlight.

Here are some steps to follow if you are going through something difficult and are wanting to let go:

- **Acknowledge the pain**

  Before anything, I had to stop pretending I was okay. I had to name what happened and to call the abuse what it was. I had to honour my own suffering without shame.

- **Accept what cannot be changed**

  No letter, no apology and no amount of closure will rewrite the past. I stopped chasing the 'why' and started focusing on *what now*.

- **Choose to forgive**

  Not because what he did was forgivable but because I refused to be defined by it anymore. I refused to be a victim my entire life. I chose to release the bitterness, not because it wasn't justified, but because it was too heavy to carry.

- **Create a ritual for release**

  Under a quiet night sky, I lit a small fire to burn the letter I wrote and watched the paper turn to ash. I encourage you to find your own ritual to let go of what you are holding on to. And in its place make space for a stillness… a clearing.

PRACTICAL EXERCISES FOR FORGIVENESS

1. Forgiveness letters: a pathway for you

If you're holding onto hurt or any part of an incident or person, I encourage you to write your own letter. Don't filter it. Don't worry about spelling or style. Write it raw, the way the pain feels. Whether it's to a parent, partner, friend or even to yourself. You don't have to send it. Just release it from your body, where it's been living too long.

Use the template below to write a letter of forgiveness to someone who hurt you — or to yourself. This letter is not meant to be sent. It's a personal exercise in release and healing.

For example:

Dear [Name _________________]

I've held onto a lot of pain, confusion and grief because of what happened between us. There were things you did or didn't do that left deep wounds. I've spent time replaying the past, trying to make sense of it all. But today, I choose to let go of the weight of this story.

I forgive you. Not because it was okay, but because I no longer want to carry this pain with me. I release myself from the anger, from the sadness, from the story that tied me to this hurt.

I may never understand your reasons. I may never receive the apology I deserve. But still, I choose peace.

I forgive you. And I am free.

Sincerely,

[Your Name_____________________________]

Use this space to write your own letter:

____

____

____

____

____

____

____

____

____

2. Journal prompts for processing forgiveness

- What memory or experience still holds emotional charge for me? Why does it continue to affect me?
- What do I wish I could say to the person who hurt me?
- How has holding onto this pain impacted my daily life or relationships?
- What part of me needs the most healing right now?
- What would it feel like to let go of this resentment?
- What lessons have I learned from this experience?
- How can I choose peace for myself, even without closure from them?

Notes:

3. Energetic release practice

Sometimes, our healing requires more than words. Try this:

- Close your eyes and imagine a cord connecting you to the person or memory that still holds pain.
- With every exhale, see that cord fray.
- With each inhale, feel strength returning to your body.
- And then, in your mind, gently cut the cord.

You are not bound to the past. Not anymore.

4. Daily affirmations for letting go

Say them out loud. Whisper them. Write them on your mirror. Make them your truth.

- I am not what happened to me.
- I am worthy of joy and tenderness.
- I choose peace over pain.
- I let go of what no longer serves me.
- I am healing, one breath at a time.
- I release the past and welcome my future.
- I forgive not to forget, but to be free.
- I forgive to set myself free.
- I am worthy of love and peace.

Write your own.

-
-
-
-
-
-
-
-
-
-
-

ON A FINAL NOTE

Healing is not about trying to forget what happened; it's about remembering who you were before the hurt and choosing to return to being that person or a different version of that person. I learned overtime that closure doesn't always come from the person who broke you; it comes from within you, from the strength you find to stop waiting for their apology and to move on and heal yourself.

In the process of letting go, I did not lose my past. I simply stopped letting it define me as a person. And in that release of emotions, I found something way more powerful than romantic love… my inner peace.

CHAPTER 8

Building healthy and happy relationships

I used to think the hardest goodbye of my life would be to the man who promised me forever but delivered a cage. It wasn't. The hardest farewell came later, when I began sorting every bond I had in my life, like friendships, family ties and even my own self-talk, through the same filter I'd once reserved for romance. I discovered how quietly toxicity can slip into the spaces between people who claim to love each other, how it can flourish in jokes that cut a little too deep or in favours tallied like debts.

It began with a harmless brunch for four. I arrived a little early, my palms damp with the kind of anxiety that's easy to mistake for excitement. When the others walked in, they hugged me and spent the next hour making snide comments about a mutual friend who wasn't there. The laughter felt bitter and I left with a stomach ache that had nothing to do with pancakes. For years I had defined this kind of banter as normal. That morning, I heard something different, the hiss of contempt wrapped in confetti. I drove home in silence, realising I'd just attended a roast disguised as fun, harmless gossip. I began to think, if they could so casually speak badly about someone they'd known far longer than me, someone who they so-called a close friend, what were they saying about me when I wasn't in the room?

I didn't know then that some of the deepest wounds could come from the people who once stood beside you in your darkest hours smiling, nodding and secretly hoping you'd never shine too bright.

The first time I felt it, truly felt it, was when I bought my first home. It was a milestone that had taken years and years of sacrifice, budget dinners, moving into a tiny space to save up. I had signed the papers, held the keys and stood alone in that empty living room with tears rolling down my cheeks not from fear or fatigue, but from an overwhelming sense of pride. This was mine. I had built this life with my own hands.

Naturally, I wanted to share it with someone who had known me through the ramen years. So I texted an old friend from uni, let's call her Mia, because she had stood beside me through most of our learning to 'adult' in life. I expected joy. I expected one of those celebratory calls or excited texts to show genuine happiness for someone you love.

Instead, her response was flat. *Yay congrats. I got a new job.*

No follow-ups. No questions. Just a swift pivot to herself. As if my success triggered some sort of internal scoreboard, and Mia needed to level the playing field. It felt like I had entered a high school competition I didn't know we were still playing. I read the message twice and replied to her success as I usually do, with congratulations and by asking more questions about it.

That moment rewired something in me. It wasn't the first time Mia had done this. I scrolled through our chat history and found a breadcrumb trail I had ignored for a long time.

Every milestone of mine was met with a shrug or a subtle dig, while every setback of hers was recited as proof that the world owed her something. These were the breadcrumbs of our history… the moments I'd dismissed as 'her being in a mood' or 'just bad timing'.

The way she would go quiet when things went well for me, or take subtle jabs masked as banter. When I got engaged years earlier, she said, 'Don't get pregnant as soon as you marry and become boring like all the other married people.' When I did well in uni or a job, she said, 'Well, you are just gifted and don't need to work hard like the rest of us.' I'd laughed. I'd brushed it off. But now I realised it. I had been minimising my own joy to make someone else comfortable.

Our friendship was a two-lane highway where I drove both cars, filled both tanks, paid both tolls. When I finally stopped calling, weeks passed before she noticed. The silence felt less like loss and more like oxygen.

Those experiences, along with my marriage, taught me love can turn carnivorous and forced me to redraw my map of intimacy. I stopped measuring relationships by their length and started measuring them by their depth and safety. I asked brutal questions regularly: does this person celebrate my joy without suspicion? Do they correct me gently when I'm wrong, or weaponise my mistakes? When I succeed, do they clap or flinch? Am I the only one carrying this relationship?

The audit was painful. Some ties frayed, while others snapped. But in the empty space that remained, I learned what healthy love sounds like… my brother scheduling regular calls because 'big sisters need checking on, too,' or a new colleague sliding coffee across the desk and saying, 'I'm proud of you,' with no asterisk attached. Or an old friend helping me navigate a new city by doing weekly check-ins and ensuring I am not lonely by constantly planning new activities for me to explore and meet new people.

I began collecting green flags the way children collect seashells:

- **Consistency**. Healthy people don't treat affection like surge pricing.
- **Curiosity**. They ask, 'How can I support you?' instead of prescribing cures.
- **Boundary literacy**. A friend who hears 'I need space' and answers 'Take what you need' is worth their weight in gold.

The truth is real love doesn't need you to be smaller. It doesn't punish you for growing. It cheers for you and even when it's hard. Even when they're not winning.

Now, when I build new relationships or try to rebuild old ones I look for softness, not performance. I notice how people respond to my boundaries. I watch how they act when the spotlight isn't on them. I listen for the sound of genuine joy in their voice when I win.

One friend sent me a card after hearing about my house. Handwritten. 'You built this with grit, I'm so damn proud of you.' I cried reading it. Not because of the words, but because I knew she meant them. Her joy didn't come with a price. It wasn't earned or measured or conditional. It just was.

Here are questions I ask myself before planting roots in new soil:

1. Do we laugh without the joke being someone's dignity?
2. Can we disagree without dishonour?
3. When one of us shines, does the other reach for sunglasses or a dimmer switch?
4. Would I trust this person with a fragile dream?

5. Could I fail spectacularly beside them and still feel safe?

If any answer falters, I slow down. Love, romantic or platonic should expand the room inside your chest, not shrink it.

I wish I could tell the woman hunched over cold coffee years ago that healthy bonds do exist; they just speak a different dialect. They sound like, *'Text me when you get home.'* They taste like soup left on a doorstep. They feel like the exact opposite of luck, because luck is random and this kind of love is intentional.

This is what I know now

Happy relationships, be it friendships, partnerships, family ties and even the ones with ourselves, aren't built on how often we talk or how long we've known each other. They're built on how free we feel to be exactly who we are, without the need to dim, apologise or edit.

Love isn't a scorecard. It's not a contest. It's a mirror, a balm and a place to land.

Today my circle is smaller, but every voice in it is a lighthouse, not a tripwire. We trade honesty like worn-out novels, pass around each other's victories, and guard one another's tenderness. Together, we've written a silent pact: no one here will ever have to earn their right to breathe freely. That, finally, is what I call home.

I no longer chase the ones who flinch when I rise. I make space for those who steady me when I fall, and cheer for me when I soar, and I ensure I do the same for them too.

Because I deserve that kind of love.

And so do you…

PRACTICE EXERCISES FOR BUILDING HEALTHY AND HAPPY RELATIONSHIPS

This exercise is designed to help you reflect on your current relationships, recognise unhealthy patterns and cultivate deeper, more supportive connections in your life.

1. Relationship inventory

Write down the names of 5–7 people you interact with regularly. For each, answer the following:

Name	How do I feel after spending time with them?	Do I feel seen and respected?	Do they support my growth?	Can I express myself without fear?

Reflection prompt: What patterns are emerging? Are there any relationships that consistently drain or energise you?

2. Green flags vs. red flags

Check what applies in your current relationships.

✓ Green flags (healthy relationship signs):

- ☐ They celebrate my wins without comparison
- ☐ They communicate openly and respectfully
- ☐ They respect my boundaries
- ☐ I feel safe being emotionally vulnerable
- ☐ They're consistent, not just present during crisis
- ☐ There's mutual effort and care
- ☐ I feel energised and lighter after spending time together

✓ Red flags (unhealthy relationship signs):

- ☐ They criticise or diminish my achievements
- ☐ I feel I have to 'shrink' or 'change myself' around them
- ☐ They make me feel guilty for setting boundaries
- ☐ There's competition instead of collaboration
- ☐ I feel emotionally drained after being with them
- ☐ They only show up when they need something
- ☐ I don't feel safe expressing myself fully

Reflection prompt: Which relationships have more red flags than green? Which ones make you feel safe, accepted and empowered?

3. Clarifying your relationship standards

Write out your non-negotiables for a healthy relationship (romantic or platonic).

1.

2.

3.

4.

5.

4. Intention setting

Choose one relationship that feels healthy and describe how you'll invest in it more intentionally.

Now, choose one relationship that feels misaligned and consider:

- What boundary do you need to set?

- Is it worth repairing or time to release?

Notes:

____

____

____

Step 5. Affirm and anchor

Affirmations:

- I am worthy of healthy, happy and respectful relationships.
- I release connections that no longer serve my highest good.
- I create space for love that uplifts and expands me.
- I attract people who meet me with honesty, joy and care.

Write your own:

- _______________________________________

- _______________________________________

- _______________________________________

- _______________________________________

ON A FINAL NOTE

The process of building healthy relationships and unlearning patterns of toxic love is never linear. For me, it was a series of quiet awakening moments when I caught myself choosing peace instead of chaos, the truth over illusion and time for growth over feelings of guilt. There will be times when you outgrow people who once felt like home to you. You will mourn friends that no longer fit, sometimes even more than you mourned an old lover. But you will find beauty in new bonds, relationships and friendships that are rooted in authenticity, kindness and mutual respect.

CHAPTER 9

The importance of boundaries and saying no

DURING MY EARLY career years, I often overextended myself to demonstrate my dedication to work. My inbox was always humming with urgency and the lines between diligence and depletion would blur without warning. On a Friday afternoon my phone vibrated incessantly with emails from colleagues, Teams messages pinging and calendar invites overlapping like waves crashing against each other. 'Can you help with this?' 'We're counting on you for that.' 'Just a quick favour…'

My reflex to say yes was almost Pavlovian. I didn't pause to consider my capacity or bandwidth. I simply opened my laptop wider, took a longer sip of my now-cold coffee, and responded with practised enthusiasm. 'Sure'. 'No problem.' 'Happy to help.'

But as the office emptied and the lights hummed above me in the quiet, a familiar heaviness settled on my chest. A slow, creeping fog that had no name but had lived with me for years. I was not just tired; I was emotionally threadbare. I felt invisible in a room where I had willingly become everyone else's solution but my own. My chest tightened with frustration. Not at the workload, but at myself.

Why did I keep saying yes when my soul was pleading for rest?

The answer was both simple and painful. I had never learned how to say NO.

The legacy we carry

I was realising that this wasn't a one-time slip; this was a pattern with me. You could even call it a lifestyle. I had spent years cultivating a reputation as the reliable one, the person who could be counted on to carry the extra load, pick up the slack and go the extra mile not just in my professional life, but also in my personal life. I wore this identity like a badge of honour, unaware that it had slowly turned into a burden too heavy to carry.

In that moment I sat still long enough to let the discomfort catch up with me. Not the discomfort of the work itself but the deeper ache and the quiet betrayal of self that had become a habit. *Why did I find it so difficult to say no? Why did self-preservation feel like a sin?*

The answers lived in the corners of my childhood. For many of us, especially those raised on praise for being 'helpful', the word 'no' feels like a betrayal. I grew up equating compliance with kindness and availability with love. I had been praised for being agreeable, applauded for keeping the peace as the older sibling, and loved for being easy to manage. I internalised early on that saying yes made me likeable, even lovable. I believed that turning down a request, any request, meant risking disapproval or worse rejection. I had never been taught that I was allowed to have needs. I had only ever learned how to meet the needs of others.

Somewhere along the way, I began to confuse boundaries with selfishness. I thought being kind meant being available at all times. I thought love meant self-sacrifice. I thought strength meant pushing through and saying yes to maintain the peace. I hadn't realised that by constantly pouring from my cup without refilling it, I was left perpetually parched.

It took years of quiet suffering and one particularly soul-weary evening to understand that what I had been missing was boundaries. Not walls to shut people out but gentle fences to protect the parts of me I had neglected. Boundaries, as I came to realise, were not about rejection; they were about self-preservation. They weren't about conflict; they were more about clarity.

What are boundaries, really?

Boundaries are not selfish, aggressive or cold. They are essential acts of self-respect with quiet declarations that we too are worthy of protection, space and peace. They are the invisible lines that define where we end and others begin.

Boundaries come in many forms:

- **Physical**: respect for your personal space and bodily autonomy.
- **Emotional**: knowing your feelings are valid and not subject to manipulation.
- **Mental**: honouring your right to think, believe and value differently from others.
- **Energetic**: recognising when someone's presence exhausts you and stepping away to recharge.

Each type serves as scaffolding for a healthy and balanced life.

For me, the first step was noticing. I started paying attention to who and what made me feel resentful. A lingering phone call from a friend who never asked how I was doing and only called or picked up the phone when she was either bored, alone or in a crisis. A meeting invitation disguised as 'a five-minute quick chat' that ended up taking my whole lunch hour. A family member who assumed I'd drop everything for them, yet again. It wasn't that I didn't care for these people. I did. But care without limits leads to depletion. Love without self-regard erodes from the inside out.

Saying 'no' without guilt

Once I could identify what was draining me, the next challenge was articulating what I needed. At first, the words felt foreign in my mouth.

'I can't take that on right now.' 'I need a moment to think about it.' 'I'm busy right now.'

Each sentence trembled like a newborn foal, unsteady and uncertain. My voice cracked, my heart raced and guilt rushed in like a flood.

But something else followed too… relief. A strange and weightless sensation. A quiet exhale. And then something miraculous happened. The world didn't end. No one screamed. No bridges burned. In fact, most people listened. Some even respected me more.

Still, the guilt lingered. The guilt for saying no. The guilt for taking up space. The guilt for honouring my limits when I had been conditioned to believe that love required limitlessness. But guilt, as I discovered, is not always a sign that you're doing something wrong. Sometimes it's simply a sign that you're doing something new.

I started journalling after every boundary I set to acknowledge my wins, no matter how small. I wrote about how my stomach knotted, how my hands shook and how I worried people would think I was difficult or cold. And I also wrote about the afterglow I felt… the deep, soul-level satisfaction of standing up for myself. The tiny spark of self-trust that ignited each time I chose honesty over obligation. I realised that guilt and growth often arrive together and that you can survive both.

Over time I built what I now think of as my boundary voice, a voice that is firm without being harsh and honest without being cruel. I rehearsed it in the mirror. I practised it with friends. I even created scripts and reminders I could fall back on when I panicked.

'That doesn't work for me.'

'Thank you but I need to decline as I have other plans.'

'I already have too much on my plate right now.'

Each phrase became an anchor in moments when old habits threatened to return.

Setting boundaries didn't just change how I related to others. It changed how I related to myself. I started scheduling time for rest the same way I would schedule a meeting. I turned off notifications after work hours. I gave myself permission to say no without explanation, to decline invitations without guilt and to leave texts unanswered if they arrived during sacred moments of solitude.

Some people drifted away. That's the truth. When you stop over-giving, those who benefited from your silence or compliance may not applaud your voice. But the people who stayed were those who met me in this new space of mutual respect bringing a depth and honesty to my life that I hadn't known was possible.

Boundaries, as I now understand them, are not about shutting the world out. They are about keeping the right things in. They are about tending to your own garden first and building a life that feels substantial and real. It's not about perfection, but presence. It's not about control, but care.

Today, I am no longer the person who reflexively says yes to everything. I am someone who pauses. Who considers. Who knows her worth isn't measured by how exhausted she is at the end of the day. I have learned that saying no is not an act of defiance but an act of devotion to myself.

This is not a mastery I have achieved, but a practice I return to daily. Each time I say no, I am saying yes to something far greater… my inner peace, my purpose, my presence. And in that sacred space I am finally free.

Building boundaries doesn't happen overnight. It is a conscious, ongoing practice. This is how I started:

1. Identify what/who drains your energy.

Start noticing what makes you feel depleted or lowers your energy; it could be some people, a place or habits you have. It could be a friend who only calls when he or she needs you but is never present to do the same for you, or it could be your manager who assumes your time is always flexible for them.

2. Define what you need.

Do you need less contact, clearer expectations or uninterrupted time for yourself? Be honest about what makes you feel safe, respected and whole.

3. Communicate with compassion.

Boundaries don't need to be loud to be powerful. Speak clearly and kindly. 'I'm not able to help with that today' is both direct and gentle or 'I appreciate the invitation, but I have to pass' is a good way too.

4. Enforce with grace and consistency.

Even when it feels awkward or guilt creeps in, stand firm. Boundaries lose their power if you abandon them the moment discomfort arises.

Since embracing boundaries, my life hasn't become easier. It's become more honest. I've shed relationships rooted in guilt and nurtured those built on mutual respect. I've become more attuned to what brings me joy and more ruthless about protecting it.

Saying no didn't close doors. It opened the right ones.

So if you're standing at the edge of burnout, exhausted by a thousand yeses that never served you, I invite you to try one small, radical act of rebellion:

Say NO today to others to finally say YES to yourself.

PRACTICAL EXERCISES FOR SETTING BOUNDARIES

Here are five beautifully crafted practical exercise templates to support you in your journey of creating and maintaining healthy boundaries. These exercises are designed to help with self-reflection, clarity, communication and practice.

1. Boundary inventory: Where am I giving too much?

Use this to identify the areas where you're overextending yourself and where boundaries are needed.

Area of life	Situation/ example	How it makes me feel	What boundary is needed
Work	Taking on extra projects after hours	Drained, unappreciated	'I am not available after 6 pm.'
Family	Sister calling daily with emotional drama	Anxious, overwhelmed	'I can talk once a week when I have capacity.'
Friendships	A friend always cancels plans last minute	Disrespected, not valued	'I need commitments to be honoured or communicated.'

| Social media | Always replying to messages immediately | Tense, reactive | 'I check DMs once a day, not constantly.' |

Add your own:

Area of life	Situation/ example	How it makes me feel	What boundary is needed

2. The 'no' script builder

Use this template to practise saying no gracefully and firmly.

Scenario: What's being asked of me?

Why I want to say no:

What I'm afraid will happen if I do:

What I will say instead:

Script examples:

- 'Thanks for thinking of me. I'm not available, but I hope it goes well.'
- 'I really appreciate the offer, but I'll have to pass this time.'
- 'I'd love to help you in the future, but I need to focus on my current commitments.'

Now create your own:

Write your personalised script:

3. Boundary communication practice

Use this role-play framework to prepare for tough conversations.

Person/ situation	What I want to say	Possible reaction	How will I stay grounded
Friend who calls only during crisis	'I care about you, but I need space after 8 pm to unwind.'	'You're being distant.'	'I'm not withdrawing. I'm taking care of myself.'
Parent who criticises	'I'm not open to feedback about my life right now.'	'I'm just trying to help.'	'I need space to make my own choices.'
Boss assigning extra work	'I don't have capacity to take this on.'	'You're not being a team player.'	'I want to deliver quality work not burnout.'

4. Boundary guilt reframe journal

Use this when guilt shows up after you've set a boundary.

What boundary did I set?

How did I feel before I set it?

How did I feel after?

What guilt or fear came up?

Is the guilt true or just familiar?

What would I tell a friend in my shoes?

New truth I choose to believe: 'Setting boundaries is not selfish, it's self-honouring.'

5. My boundaries manifesto

Create your personal guide to the boundaries you're committed to protecting.

> Dear Myself,
>
> 'I, ______________________________, commit to protecting my time, energy and emotional well-being.
>
> Here are the boundaries I choose to honour in my life:'
>
> I will no longer say yes out of guilt or fear of disapproval.
>
> I will take time to rest and unplug without explanation.
>
> I will not engage in conversations that drain or disrespect me.
>
> I will protect my peace by stepping away when needed.
>
> I will speak my truth even when it's uncomfortable.
>
> Add your own:
>
> Signed with love,
>
> **[Your Name]**
>
> Date: ______________________

ON A FINAL NOTE

Every yes you give up thoughtlessly steals from the yes you may give to something meaningful for you. Your health. Your children. Your art. Your dreams. Your peace of mind.

Saying no is not selfish.

It's sacred.

It's the way we reclaim our lives from the dictatorship of obligation.

It's how we educate the world about how to treat us, not through anger or withdrawal but through quiet clarity.

And sometimes, the kindest thing you can do for yourself and for others is simply to say: **'No.'**

CHAPTER 10

Navigating loss and finding joy again

It was a Tuesday the day that my father died. I was sitting in a glass-walled conference room halfway across the world from my family home, surrounded by spreadsheets, stale coffee and the dull hum of fluorescent lighting. The office was sterile and modern, located in the middle of nowhere in suburban Sydney.

I had just finished presenting at a steering committee meeting to a room full of executives when I noticed my phone buzzing relentlessly. First, one missed call. Then another. Then a message from my brother.

'Call me. It's urgent.'

I excused myself, heart pounding. Somewhere between the hallway and the stairs, I already knew. Sometimes the soul hears what the ears have not yet confirmed.

When I finally called back, my mum's voice cracked.

'He's gone.'

Just like that.

The man who raised me, who taught me how to ride a

bike, to tie my shoelaces, to stand tall when life tried to knock me down, was no longer alive.

The fluorescent lights above me suddenly felt too bright, the office too quiet. And I felt too far away from home. I rushed out of the office after letting my boss know, who kindly offered to make some flight bookings for me immediately.

I felt like a ghost in my own body, numbness wrapping around me like an old blanket. I didn't cry right away. Instead, there was a stillness. A silent scream in my chest. I wandered around my apartment aimlessly, my mind jumping between memories and regrets. I should have asked him more about his childhood. I should have called more often. I should have said 'I love you' without rushing to hang up. I shouldn't have had that argument with him the last time I saw him. The guilt was a tide pulling me under.

For weeks after I returned from the funeral I drifted through life in a fog. Friends tried to reach out but their words felt foreign and distant. My laughter turned brittle and moments of joy felt like betrayals against the memory of my dad. It was as if a part of me had been severed, a constant ache echoing in the silence he left behind.

I kept going through the motions of working, socialising and showing up, but I was a ghost in my own life. I'd smile, but it was hollow. I'd eat, but I couldn't taste. The joy I once felt in little things like the morning sunlight on the curtains and the warmth of tea in my palms had been replaced by numbness. There is a particular kind of grief that comes when you're expected to carry on after such a loss, when you are overseas and far away from family, battling loneliness all alone. I cried myself to sleep sometimes, without any particular reason, and I realised that grief doesn't always shout. Sometimes it's silent, polite and haunting.

What I lost wasn't just my father; it was all the future moments that would now never be. I mourned the man, yes. But I also mourned the unspoken words, the unfinished conversations, the version of me that only existed when he was still here.

Months later, the first time I really laughed again it took me by surprise. I was at brunch with friends. Someone made a joke about dating in our thirties and I threw my head back and laughed until my sides hurt. And then suddenly guilt crept it. Crushing, immediate guilt.

How could I laugh when my father was no longer alive?

I excused myself and cried in the bathroom. But later something shifted. I remembered my dad's laughter and started thinking about some happy moments with him. I remembered how he used to nudge me and say, 'Life is too short to take seriously. Even grief needs a break.' I remembered how he, while battling with Parkinson's disease for most of his life, was always trying to live it up. I realised that finding joy wasn't a betrayal. It was a tribute.

However, grief doesn't come with a manual or map like it does in a psychology textbook. It's not five stages in a straight line. It's circular. Chaotic. Healing and hurting often coexist. One morning I'd wake up feeling at peace, ready to start again. The next I'd crumble because I heard a song he loved.

Some days I felt nothing. Other days, I felt everything.

I had to learn that these fluctuations were okay. That joy didn't replace grief; it partnered with it. That healing wasn't about 'moving on', but rather, moving *forward* with the memory.

What helped me heal
1. A memory altar, far from home

In a quiet corner of my apartment, I created a memory space. It was a personal item I had brought back with me from my father's wardrobe back home. Some nights, I sat and looked at it and lit a candle or just spoke to it in my head.

2. Letter writing

I wrote a letter to him, a long and rambling letter about my feelings and what I was struggling with. I told him things I never had the chance to say. I asked him questions I knew he'd never answer. I told him about the people or future moments I feel he will be missing during my life. And somehow this ritual stitched up tiny tears in my heart.

3. Walking without purpose

I started walking every evening with no phone or destination. Just me and the fresh air, with nature making space for my sorrow without judgement. Trees didn't flinch when I cried beneath them. The sky didn't mind when I was silent for hours. Nature simply witnessed and that was enough.

4. Permission slips

Each morning, I wrote myself a small slip of paper, giving myself permission to feel what I needed most.

- *I give myself permission to grieve slowly.*
- *I give myself permission to laugh without guilt.*
- *I give myself permission to miss him every single day.*

These slips weren't magic, but they reminded me that healing isn't about performing strength. It's about allowing all the messy emotions their rightful place.

PRACTICAL EXERCISES FOR HEALING THROUGH A LOSS

1. Letter ritual

Write a letter to the person you've lost. Be raw. Say the things you couldn't. Express anything you didn't get to say. Share memories, regrets, gratitude and love. Don't worry about structure, just write from your heart. Then try writing a letter *from* them to you. What would they say if they could still guide you? Keep it somewhere private, return to it whenever you need comfort.

2. Build your own memory space

Create a small altar like corner or wall or a drawer with a photo or any personal items and things that remind you of your loved one. It could be photos, objects, scents. Visit it whenever you feel the need. It becomes a touchstone when the world feels distant.

My memory space plan:

3. Daily permission slips

Each day, write yourself a permission slip. Consider the examples described in the above chapter.

Write your own permission slips below:

4. Joy jar reflections

Place a jar somewhere visible. Every time something makes you smile, no matter how small, write it down on a small slip of paper and place it inside. Over time you'll build a physical reminder that joy still exists even in the middle of grief.

Use the space below to record your joyful moments today.

5. Grief walk reflection

Take a walk without distractions. Let your thoughts flow naturally. After your walk, use the space below to write about what came up for you.

What I noticed or felt:

6. Affirmations for healing

Choose or write some affirmations to carry you through difficult days.

- I am healing in my own time and in my own way.
- It's okay to feel joy again.
- Grief is a reflection of love, and both can coexist.

Write your own affirmations below:

ON A FINAL NOTE

It took nearly two years, but I remember the first day I freely danced again. It was in my living room alone and barefoot with music turned too loud. I laughed and cried at once.

Because joy had finally returned not to erase the grief but to sit beside it.

Love as I learned doesn't end. It transforms. It weaves itself into new moments, into different skies, into the sound of your own voice when you tell their story. Grief reshaped me but it did not steal the possibility of joy.

And so I live. For him. For me. For the memory of love that does not die when a heart stops beating.

PART 4

HAPPINESS AT WORK AND IN PURPOSE

CHAPTER 11

Finding purpose beyond pay checks

No one warns you that the dream you've been working so hard towards might not feel like home when you actually get it. No one warns that your shiny pay check can become a golden cage that traps you in a life that might look perfect on paper, but feels helplessly hollow in your soul.

So the day I received my first six-figure salary, I should have felt glorious as I stood on the balcony of my high-rise apartment, glass of red wine in hand, staring at the city skyline. After all, wasn't this what I had worked so hard for?

I had brushed aside so many things as I dedicated myself to the job. After all I had KPIs to hit. Clients to impress. A reputation to uphold. I had missed one of my closest friend's weddings because of a project go-live. I had forgotten a very old and dear friend's birthday two years in a row because I was 'too swamped'.

I had also brushed it aside when my doctor quietly pointed out that chronic migraines and extreme skin allergies weren't normal and that maybe my body was whispering what my mind refused to hear.

I remember sitting in a quarterly review watching my manager praise my numbers while barely registering the burnout behind my eyes. That night I returned home and stood in my kitchen staring at a sink full of dishes and a calendar packed with meetings and I whispered to no one in particular, *'Is this it?'*

I felt like I had climbed a mountain only to realise I was on the wrong peak.

What haunted me wasn't failure; it was the success that didn't feel like success.

I didn't quit immediately. I didn't book a one way ticket to Bali or become a digital nomad overnight. Instead I started small. I read – a lot… Parker Palmer, Viktor Frankl, Elizabeth Gilbert, Paulo Coelho. That's when I signed up for the mindset coaching and returned to the journalling I had once cherished. I asked uncomfortable questions. I cried.

I peeled back the layers of my life until I began to rediscover parts of myself I had long buried. The girl who loved stories, who found joy in mentoring interns, who once dreamed of building something that mattered not just something that sold.

What if my life could be driven by meaning instead of metrics?

What if my legacy wasn't the size of my pay check, but the size of my impact?

I was seeking to find my own deeper purpose.

What is purpose for you?

We often talk about purpose like it's a destination – a single 'aha' moment in your life. But for me, my purpose arrived quietly like morning light creeping through the blinds.

It showed up in unexpected places like talking to a friend

about a career or life roadblock and coming up with solutions together or writing plans that no one paid for; and mentoring younger colleagues not because I had to, but because I loved seeing them grow. Slowly, my joy returned. Not because I made more money. But because I started honouring what made me feel most alive.

Your life purpose, as I realised, isn't about abandoning your job, it's about showing up with intention.

Sometimes we confuse passion with purpose. I did too, and I'm sure most people have at some point in their life.

What I know now is that passion flares, but purpose anchors.

Passion can be the spark that gets you started but purpose is what sustains you when things get hard. Passion asks, 'What excites me?' Purpose asks, 'What matters most, even when it's not exciting?'

The two often meet. But they are not the same.

For me, purpose was about a transition from performance to contribution. From living to please others to living my truth. From competing for titles to competing for impact.

As I went through this journey, I learned that purpose did not necessarily have to mean monumental changes or heroic performances; it could be cultivated in the simple everyday acts of kindness, connection and actual living. I refocused my energy on aligning my work more closely with the values that resonated most with me, particularly those related to authenticity and community. Work gradually became less about tasks and more about building bridges of understanding and connection with people. Every interaction and all seemingly mundane assignments were opportunities to infuse my day with meaning.

For anyone who finds themselves stuck in a job that merely pays the bills, this shift in perspective is vital. It is not always about abandoning your comfort zone or quitting your job; it is about rewiring what success means for you. For me, I found that purpose was not a dramatic or epiphanic moment. It was an ongoing discovery that involved an unpredictable balancing act between personal and professional satisfaction.

In differentiating passion from purpose, I found a liberating truth. Passion may briefly spark excitement, but purpose is the steady fire that sustains us through life's inevitable ebbs and flows. True fulfilment does not lie in the external markers of wealth and achievement, but in the deeply rooted rich connections we make along the way.

If you're reading this…

If you're standing where I once stood, accomplished yet unfulfilled. Please note this: you are not broken. You are just waking up.

And that awakening is sacred.

You don't need to quit your job tomorrow. You don't need to have it all figured out. You just need to start listening. To your restlessness. To your curiosity. To the small inner voice whispering, 'There's more.'

Because there *is* more. And it's waiting for you…

As you embark on your own path to discovering happiness beyond the pay check, remember that your journey is uniquely yours. Embrace the small exercises such as a moment of reflection here, a candid chat there, as stepping stones towards a richer and more meaningful life. Your narrative is waiting to be rewritten, with each chapter filled with the beauty of authenticity and the power of genuine human connection.

May you find, as I eventually did, that the true measure of success lies in the quiet moments of introspection and the enduring relationships that sustain us long after the fleeting high of a pay check has faded into memory.

PRACTICAL EXERCISES FOR DISCOVERING PURPOSE BEYOND THE PAY CHECK

Here are three exercises I used to help shift from survival mode to soul alignment.

1. Core values compass

Step 1: Write down 10 values that are important to you (e.g. freedom, connection, creativity, service).

1. _______________________________________

2. _______________________________________

3. _______________________________________

4. _______________________________________

5. _______________________________________

6. _______________________________________

7. _______________________________________

8. _______________________________________

9. _______________________________________

10. _______________________________________

Step 2: Circle or highlight your top 3 core values.

Top 3 values:

1. ____

2. ____

3. ____

Step 3: Reflect on how these values show up in your life and work today.

Tip: Purpose often emerges where your values and actions align.

Reflection:

____

____

____

____

____

____

2. Spark inventory

When do you feel most alive?

Use the chart below to list moments from your week or month that made time disappear.

Notice patterns. What themes emerge?

These 'sparks' often hold clues to your deeper purpose.

Activity	How it makes me feel	Why it matters to me

Activity	How it makes me feel	Why it matters to me

3. Eulogy reflection

Imagine it's your 80th birthday and someone is giving a toast about your life. What legacy do you want to leave behind?

This reframes your life from the lens of meaning, not milestones.

What do you hope they say about you?

____

____

____

____

Now ask yourself: What small change can I make today to live more in alignment with this vision?

Action step:

____

____

____

____

____

____

ON A FINAL NOTE

Your purpose isn't something you will find in a job promotion, the income you earn or the amount of followers you have on social media. It's found in the quiet courage to live your truth in any situation. It's in the way you show up when no one is watching. It's about what lights a fire in your soul, even if it never makes the headlines or is something not directly related to your pay check or income.

And perhaps that's the real pay check: a life that is rich in meaning strung together by daily acts of choosing what matters the most for YOU.

CHAPTER 12

Creating joyful work

I USED TO believe my purpose had to be loud.

It had to arrive with the feeling of a standing ovation, like fireworks in my chest, and it would come stamped with a big business mission statement or a corner office view. I thought it would show up in a job title or as a significant leap to something more, something next, something that would finally prove I had made it.

But purpose as I've learned isn't always grand. Sometimes it doesn't announce itself with applause; it just whispers quietly in ordinary moments.

Mine whispered on an ordinary Wednesday.

One of those moments where everything shifts

I was walking back from a meeting, my head full of project deadlines and half-composed emails, when one of my junior colleagues approached my desk. She had just delivered her first presentation. Her voice trembled just a little, and her slides were slightly awkward, but her effort was very evident.

'Thank you for trusting in me when I didn't trust myself,' she said.

I experienced a sense of pride and joy that stirred something deep within me.

It wasn't the numbers we reached or the milestones achieved in the project; it was that moment that felt so real and authentic. That's when I understood my purpose wasn't in the job description. It was in the way I showed up for someone else and motivated them to do better. It was in the connections I built. It was in care.

Before that day, work had become a silent grind for me.

Each morning started with a sense of dread, with the weight of constant expectations on my chest before even opening my laptop. I checked boxes, achieved targets and smiled in meetings. To the outside world, I was a success. But inside, I was disappearing.

Late one night when I was feeling very tired and run down, I was searching my drawer for something and found a forgotten notebook full of doodles, quotes and sketches from the time when I still thought work could be happy. A time when I saw creativity as a 'need' rather than a 'nice to have', when curiosity drove my ideas and connection gave them wings.

That old notebook proved to be my handbook. I decided to stop waiting for happiness and start building it instead.

My first act of rebellion was small; I swapped dead data tables for visual storytelling in my reports and presentations. I began brainstorming sessions where we played with post-it notes like jigsaw pieces instead of drowning in spreadsheets. I brought art into analysis, empathy into feedback and colour into grey routines.

It wasn't just about making things 'fun'; it was about

making them real. It was about remembering why I wanted to do this work in the first place.

I also drew new boundaries. No more weekend 'quick wins' or late-night check-ins. I said 'no' kindly but firmly so I could say 'yes' to my well-being. Slowly I began to feel like myself again.

I stopped asking, 'What is my purpose?' as if it were a job listing that I hadn't yet found. Instead, I started asking, 'Where do I feel most alive?' It was the same question I had used to assess my other life areas, so why not my professional life too?

That question changed everything.

I realised purpose isn't something you chase but rather it's something you create. It's not one big moment. It's the quiet decision to align your work with your truth. To speak with intention. To listen with presence. To create beauty even when no one is watching.

I found purpose in small and almost invisible moments:

- Helping a colleague feel heard during a tough week.
- Writing a kind message in the middle of a stressful project.
- Mentoring my team to grow to their full potential and providing them with the opportunities to do so.
- Taking five extra minutes to add clarity and care to a confusing email.
- Picking up the phone to check in on your team which has nothing to do with work.

These were not acts of brilliance but they were acts of meaning.

How do you define joy?

For me, joy doesn't always scream. Sometimes it hums quietly beneath the noise of your calendar.

It appears when you're fully immersed in a flow state and in your creative zone, collaborating with a team that laughs and dreams together, or solving a problem that no one else has noticed but you.

But joy isn't guaranteed. It must be designed. Here's how I began designing it.

1. Morning mindset rituals

    I started my days by setting an intention. Not a to-do list but a to-feel list. I asked:
    What energy do I want to bring into today for myself and my team?

2. Midday joy breaks

    A beach walk. A favourite playlist. A five-minute breathing ritual. A quick stretching routine. These resets became lifelines.

3. Evening reflections

    Instead of ending the day with fatigue, I paused to celebrate what went well, even the tiniest victories. A regular evening conversation in my household became a discussion about what we achieved that day. It was sometimes as small as clearing my inbox or going to the shops to get groceries.

These rituals weren't productivity hacks. They were healing.

The power of micro purpose

When I was younger, I believed purpose was a mountain to climb. Now I know it's the path beneath your feet. It's not a destination but it's a direction and a way of living.

We often seek purpose in external validation but what if the real question is:

How do I want to feel while I work? Fulfilled? Aligned? Joyful?

Even the smallest choices can point you back to yourself.

The spark is already in you

Creating joyful work doesn't necessarily require changing your job; it requires you to return to what makes you feel alive.

Purpose is not just the why behind your work. It's the how. The who you choose to be in each moment.

Joy is not a reward. It's a practice. A rebellion. A way of honouring yourself even when the world tells you to perform instead of feel.

You don't need to wait for a promotion, a perfect opportunity or a grand revelation.

Start where you are.

Infuse your tasks with meaning.

Bring warmth into your meetings.

Say yes to the projects that light you up and no to the ones that drain your soul.

Speak your truth. Offer your heart. Create your art whether that's in spreadsheets or strategy decks or storyboards.

And one day maybe on another ordinary Wednesday, you'll feel that quiet spark again, the one that says:

This matters.

You matter.

You are exactly where you're meant to be.

Because joy and purpose were never waiting at the end of the road.

They are the road.

PRACTICAL EXERCISES FOR CREATING JOYFUL WORK

To get you started here are some practical tools for creating joyful work and rediscovering purpose.

1. 'I feel most alive when…' list

Set a timer for 10 minutes and complete the sentence:

'I feel most alive when I'm…'

Don't judge. Just write as many activities as you can. These are your purpose clues.

- ____

- ____

- ____

- ____

- ____

- ____

- ____

- ____

- ____

2. Joy audit

Draw two columns. Then ask:

How can I do more of what energises me? What can I reshape, delegate or drop?

Review weekly.

Here is an example from my journal:

Energises me	Drains me
Collaborative brainstorming	Long, agenda-less meetings
Mentoring or coaching others	Last-minute admin work
Creative presentation design	Repetitive reporting

Write yours now:

Energises me	Drains me

3. Your personal definition of success

Forget corporate ladders. Write your own 'success statement'.

Example: 'Success is feeling proud of how I treat people and how I show up, even on hard days.'

My definition of success:

____

____

____

4. Micro purpose journal

Each day write down one meaningful moment at work. Over time these will form a mosaic of your truest values in action.

Below is a space for your next 5 days.

Day 1 – A moment of meaning:

____

____

____

Day 2 – A moment of meaning:

____

____

____

Day 3 – A moment of meaning:

Day 4 – A moment of meaning:

Day 5 – A moment of meaning:

---

5. Create a 'Purpose Project'

It could be starting a wellness circle, mentoring juniors or proposing a sustainability initiative. Pick one cause that lights you up and begin there.

Think of one initiative or task at work that excites or aligns with your values. Use this space to brainstorm and commit to small actions.

Idea:

Why it matters:

First small step:

ON A FINAL NOTE

You don't need to find a new job, a new boss or make a radical change in your life to begin. You just need to listen closely to the feeling of joy in your heart and follow it, one small step at a time.

Because joyful work isn't a luxury only the rich can afford.

It's a powerful act of reclaiming yourself.

And purpose… it's never lost. It's always there, quiet, steady and waiting for you to remember.

Make today the day you choose joy, not at the end of a journey, but as a path in itself.

PART 5

HAPPINESS IN HEALTH AND WELL-BEING

CHAPTER 13

Listening to my body: a journey to wellness

Sometimes in life the most profound transformation doesn't begin with a revelation, it begins with a breakdown. I have shared many stories and moments of rebuilding my mindset, finding joy and realigning my life with purpose. But before any of that was possible, something had to come undone. This chapter takes us back to that initial unravelling moment, a moment in my life when my body whispered what I refused to hear until it finally screamed. This chapter is what shaped all of those moments of epiphany that followed.

The sun hung low in the sky as I strolled through the vibrant streets of Macau, with its colours and sounds blurring into a haze. I had spent months juggling work deadlines and personal commitments while pushing through fatigue as if it were an old friend. Each day, I filled my schedule to the brim convinced that busyness equated to worthiness. I felt invincible until that day a creeping fatigue took hold, whispering warnings I had ignored for a long time.

The following morning my body revolted. A sudden wave

of weakness crashed over me and I struggled to lift my head from the pillow. My ex-husband's voice seemed distant as he urged me to get up.

'Charu, we've got a whole city to explore!'

But I could barely muster a response. That was when the panic set in that something was very wrong.

What happened in Macau didn't begin in Macau. It began several months earlier with a fatigue that clung to my skin like humidity. I couldn't shake it. One doctor diagnosed me with glandular fever and prescribed rest, fluids and patience. But I wasn't ready to listen. I didn't want stillness. I wanted answers that aligned with my own agenda. So I brought my research to another doctor, confident that I could outwit the warning signs.

Their verdict? 'Nothing abnormal.' A green light to keep pushing.

And so I did.

I sprinted through life with a calendar choked with deadlines and decisions. Work was demanding, yes, but so was the wedding of my dreams. A grand Indian celebration that, if you know, you know. Multi-day ceremonies involving cross-continental travel, detailed planning, family politics, outfit fittings, weight-loss goals, where everything had to be perfect.

I set a goal to lose 10 kilograms in two months. Between crash dieting, overtraining and anxiety fuelled late nights, I squeezed myself into the mould of a beaming bride. But behind the smile, I was breaking. Each moment, every flight itinerary, every pre-wedding event and every family drama was another layer of depletion masked with lipstick.

Still I told myself, 'Just hold on. Just make it to Macau [the last minute honeymoon that I did not want but was planned by my ex anyways]. That's your break. That's when you'll breathe again.'

But rest delayed is rest denied.

There is a very rightful saying that if you don't make time for rest your body will make you do it.

The night before we flew to Macau my body sent another warning. A wave of illness knocked me flat. I ended up at the doctor's office begging for a quick fix. A few shots, some strong medication and I convinced myself I'd be fine. I boarded the plane like a soldier, exhausted but determined. I wouldn't let 'a little sickness' steal my hard-earned getaway.

But the rebellion was already underway.

On our first morning in Macau, I couldn't lift my head from the pillow. My ex stood over me, concern etched across his face. He ordered room service, thinking maybe I just needed to eat. I reached for a croissant but my hand wouldn't move. My fingers slackened. The pastry slipped from my grasp.

'Charu, are you okay?' he asked, voice low with fear.

I wanted to nod. I wanted to pretend. But I couldn't. My muscles that were once so quick to respond now felt submerged in cement.

The day I stopped pretending

In the space of 48 hours I went from fatigued to paralysed. The doctors ran test after test. Then the verdict came. Guillain-Barré Syndrome. A rare autoimmune disorder where the body's immune system attacks the nervous system. My own body had turned on me.

I was admitted to the ICU with a collapsed lung and failing mobility. Machines breathed for me, spoke for me and kept me alive. And all I could do was lie there mute, terrified and hollow.

There's a particular kind of grief that comes when your body betrays you. I stared at the sterile ceiling tiles trying to make sense of my new reality. Every beep from the monitors echoed like a siren in my bones.

But strangely in the middle of this panic state something opened. For the first time in years, there was no noise. No plans. No proving. Just silence. Just survival.

And with that silence came awareness.

Lying motionless in the ICU I began to hear my body not in the language of emergency but in the gentle and aching whisper it had always used. Please listen to me.

It took a month in ICU before I could sit upright with help. Another two before I could stand with help. Six months before I could walk unaided. And in those long and humbling months, I began to heal not just physically but spiritually.

I had to unlearn everything I thought I knew about strength.

I turned to practices I once rolled my eyes at, calling them 'woo woo'. Acupuncture helped release pain I didn't even know I carried. Breathwork taught me how to stay present through fear. I replaced my caffeine fuelled mornings with hydration and gratitude.

I stumbled upon the world of biohacking, not the extreme, Silicon Valley kind, but gentle, intuitive tweaks that honoured my body's rhythm. Morning sunlight helped reset my circadian clock. Magnesium soaks calmed my nervous system. I walked barefoot in the sand, reconnecting with the earth. I traded weight-loss goals for nourishment, such as leafy greens, fermented foods and seeds, which made my body hum with thankfulness.

And I wrote. Each morning, I journalled what I felt

physically, emotionally, spiritually. I noticed which people drained me, which habits hurt me, which foods supported me. I finally stopped asking my body to keep up and started asking what it needed to heal.

No bounce backs, only becoming…

There was no dramatic turning point. No montage of triumphant music. Just slow and sacred steps forward. I cried when I couldn't hold a fork. I laughed when I took my first walk to the mailbox. I wept when I could go to the toilet by myself. I celebrated every inch of progress like it was Everest.

And eventually against all odds, I made a full recovery. The doctors told me that was rare.

But it was still just the beginning. It took years and years to change my lifestyle and learn how to truly listen to my body. I no longer chase perfection. I don't follow rigid diets or trends. Instead, I follow my body's cues. I practise a few core biohacking habits and cultivate space for rest. Wellness, I've learned, is not the absence of illness. It's the presence of compassion. Over the years, biohacking concepts I have learned have immensely assisted me in my journey.

Essentially, biohacking is the art of consciously optimising your body and mind. It combines lifestyle design, nutrition, technology and self-testing to optimise your life in order to live longer, think more clearly and have more energy. You can imagine it as having a high-performance car that you tweak the gas, tune and add modifications to so that it runs at top capacity.

Here is a little cheat sheet with some easy changes that helped me over the past few years. Perhaps they can help you too.

1. Light is medicine

- Morning: Get 10 minutes of natural sunlight within an hour of waking up. It helps to reset your system.
- Evening: Dim lights, block blue light and avoid screens 1 hour before bed.

2. Food as fuel

- Choose organic whole foods, high-quality fats (avocado, olive oil, grass-fed butter), grass-fed meat and poultry and ethically wild caught fish.
- Cut refined sugar and ultra processed foods out of your regular diet.
- Intermittent fasting is great but for women, adjust fasting windows around your cycle (shorter fasts during luteal phase).

3. Hydration upgrade

- Add a pinch of sea salt or electrolytes to water for better hydration.
- Drink at least 2–3 litres of water daily.
- Instead of caffeine, start your day with water. I like drinking a warm cup of water with lemon before my morning coffee.

4. Stress reset

- Use breathwork techniques like Box Breathing or the
  4-7-8 Method once or twice daily.

  Box Breathing is a calming technique where you
  breath in for 4 seconds or counts, hold for 4, exhale
  for 4 and hold again for 4 seconds like tracing the
  sides of a square box with your breath.
  4 min – 7 min – 8 min breathing is a relaxation
  method based on the ratio of 4:7:8 breaths for
  inhaling, holding and exhaling, respectively.

- Practise grounding with barefoot contact with
  the earth for 5 to 10 minutes. It can be a walk in
  the park on the grass, beach walk or just in your
  backyard.

5. Move smart, not more

- Lift heavy (safely) once or twice a week for longevity.
- Add short bursts of HIIT. Keep cardio minimal but
  intentional. I prefer long and consistent walks over
  running.

6. Sleep like it's sacred

- Sleep in a cool room (~18°C).
- No caffeine after 3 pm.
- Use blackout curtains or an eye mask.

7. Cycle aware adjustments (for women) *

- Follicular phase: push harder in workouts, experiment with fasting.
- Luteal phase: prioritise rest, gentle movement and nourishing carbs.

8. Mindset and tracking

- Journal daily your energy, mood and sleep quality to spot trends.

Choose one biohack at a time and stick with it for 2–4 weeks before layering more. Small changes, compounded over time, create the greatest transformation.

*More on cycle aware adjustment for women:

The menstrual cycle has four phases that are most dominant and each of them affects a woman's energy, mood and body in unique ways. Think about it in terms of the seasons of the month:

1. Menstrual phase (period) or 'winter'

   - Days: ~1–5 (depending on individual)
   - What's going on: the uterine lining is shedding, that is when there is bleeding.
   - How you feel: energy is lowest, mood can be subdued and the body needs rest.
   - Best hacks: sleep more, eat warm and nutritious food, exercise lightly like walking or stretching.

2. Follicular phase or 'spring'

   - Days: ~6–13 (following period, up to ovulation)

- What's going on: ovarian follicles develop eggs; estrogen starts rising.
- How you feel: energy builds, mood lifts, creativity and focus increase.
- Best hacks: try new projects, exercise more vigorously and attempt longer fasting or cutting back on meals as your body can heal more quickly here.

3. Ovulation phase or 'summer'

- Days: ~14–16 (mid-cycle, but varies in timing)
- What's going on: the egg is released; hormones surge (estrogen, testosterone and luteinising hormone).
- How you feel: lots of energy, confidence and typically the most sociable phase.
- Best hacks: great time for high-intensity exercise, significant meetings or celebrations. Eat lighter, raw foods to supplement the body's energy.

4. Luteal phase or 'autumn'

- Days: ~17–28 (after ovulation up to the next period).
- What's going on: progesterone rises to prepare your body for a possible pregnancy. If pregnancy does not occur your hormone levels drop towards the end.
- How you feel: first half (early luteal) = steady energy; second half (late luteal, i.e. PMS) = energy dips, mood swings, hunger or cravings, bloating and tiredness may be experienced.

- Top hacks: rest more, eat more complex carbohydrates (like sweet potato, oats), reduce caffeine and prioritise calming activities like yoga, journalling or deep breathing.

PRACTICAL EXERCISES FOR RECONNECTING WITH YOUR BODY

If you're reading this and wondering how to start listening to your body, here are some gentle, and grounding tools I use.

1. Daily check-ins

Take five quiet minutes in the morning and evening. Ask yourself:

- How does my body feel right now?
- What is it asking for?
- What am I ignoring?

Morning reflection:

____

____

____

Evening reflection:

____

____

____

2. Body scan meditation

Lie down, start simple breathing in and out with your nose. Breathe slowly. Move your attention from your toes to your head. Notice tension, temperature or any sensation. Offer each part presence not judgement.

Body scan notes:

3. Energy logging

Keep a journal to track:

- Foods you eat
- Activities you engage in
- Emotional state
- Energy levels (1–10)

Patterns will emerge. They will teach you.

Daily template:

Time	Food/activity	Emotion	Energy (1–10)

4. Joyful movement

Forget the gym if it feels like punishment. Move in ways that bring joy. Dance, stretch, walk, swim. Let movement be medicine, not obligation.

Activities:

____

____

____

____

Reflections on how it felt:

____

____

____

____

5. Micro restoratives

Every 90 minutes, pause to:

- Stand up
- Breathe deeply (3 breaths)
- Drink water with a pinch of rock salt
- Gently stretch

These tiny rituals build nervous system resilience over time.

ON A FINAL NOTE

Your body is not your opponent. It's your oldest ally. Your first home. It remembers every joy, every ache and every secret you've tried to outrun. It is not asking for perfection. Only presence.

Now I walk slower. I rest often. I laugh deeper. I eat what feels like sunlight. And when my body whispers I try to listen. Because I know, it's not just speaking. It's leading me home.

This chapter is your invitation. Not to hustle harder. But to soften. To listen. And to return to the ancient and sacred knowing that your health, your happiness and your life were never meant to be sacrificed.

CHAPTER 14

Creating space with mindfulness and balance

THE CHAOS OF my mornings used to feel like a never ending run on quicksand. I'd wake up with a jolt, no gentle rising, no soft stretches or birdsong, just the shrill bark of my alarm. It dragged me from restless sleep like a rope over gravel. I'd stumble into the bathroom phone in hand to brush my teeth while skimming emails, already mentally rehearsing meetings, errands and responsibilities. By the time the kettle boiled, my to-do list had already stretched into the evening.

Burned toast, unread texts and sometimes mismatched socks. Breath came in short bursts. My chest felt tight. My heart pounding. And still I smiled, proud of my productivity. Proud of how much I could juggle before even starting my day at work.

Yet beneath the adrenaline was something quieter and far more dangerous. It was a feeling of disconnection.

I didn't notice it at first. It crept in subtly like fog inching across a landscape. I was doing everything I thought I was supposed to... achieving, performing, producing, but I felt hollow inside. My body moved, my mouth spoke, but my spirit… it lingered somewhere behind, begging me to be acknowledged.

It was only after my father's death, when the kind of grief that settles in your bones shook me to pieces, that I began to notice the silence and pain behind the busyness.

And that silence terrified me.

When stillness hurts before it heals

The first time I tried mindfulness, or meditation as some people refer to it, I felt like a fraud. I sat cross-legged on the bedroom floor with my back rigid and eyes closed. I had imagined calm transcendence and maybe even wisdom. But what came instead was noise, lots of relentless noise. Grocery lists. Deadlines. Regrets. My mind felt like a freeway at rush hour with no exits or rest stops.

I couldn't breathe past the static.

But I stayed. Just for five minutes. I focused on my breath. Inhale for four counts. Hold. Exhale for six. Again. And again.

The storm didn't pass but the winds softened. The walls loosened inside of me. In the small space between breaths, I found something tender and that was awareness.

That night I went for a walk around the block under the quiet hush of the streetlights. Each footfall was a meditation; I made sure I was aware of the walk and not focusing on my phone. My grief followed me like a shadow but I welcomed it. I let the weight of memory press down on my steps. I didn't run from it. I just walked with it. And somehow that helped.

The myth of multitasking

I'm not sure when or where this started, but somewhere along the way, we (humans) began to equate multitasking with competence and even superiority. We praise the person who can answer emails while making breakfast, hold a meeting while replying to texts or plan a wedding while closing quarterly targets. We've turned divided attention into a badge of honour to prove that we are capable, desirable and successful. I was one of them. Remember – I called myself the Queen of Multitasking.

However, I've come to realise now that multitasking is a myth, one where we are not doing many things well. We are doing many things poorly, constantly fracturing our awareness, diluting our presence and depleting our energy.

True awareness, the kind cultivated through mindfulness is not compatible with multitasking. It asks us to slow down and attend to what's in front of us. When we do that something incredible happens for us. Our minds become quiet as our nervous system relaxes, allowing us to finally hear ourselves.

There is power in focus. In listening deeply to one conversation. In tasting one bite of food. In hearing one breath as it fills your lungs. The clarity, peace and creativity that arises in those moments is the very antidote to the scattered chaos we've normalised.

The moment I truly understood how far I'd come in cultivating awareness arrived during the most ordinary of exchanges. I was fully absorbed in a task when my partner asked me to look into something for him. Calmly, I replied, 'I need to focus on what I'm doing right now. Can it wait?'

He chuckled. 'What happened to the Queen of Multitasking? Can't juggle a few things anymore?'

And just like that it hit me.

I smiled, not at his remark but at the quiet truth behind it. I couldn't multitask anymore, not because I'd lost the ability but because I had finally trained myself not to. I had been so intentional about practising presence, so deliberate in rewiring my mind to slow down and stay in the moment, that the chaos of multitasking no longer felt natural. It felt like noise.

That realisation filled me with a deep and contented happiness. My hard work had taken root. I wasn't just learning awareness… I was finally living it.

Redefining balance

We often treat balance as a formula or a recipe, consisting of equal parts work and play, mixed with equal parts effort and rest. But true balance, as I've learned, isn't about symmetry; it's about alignment. It's about giving ourselves permission to be fully present even when life is messy.

For me, balance meant letting go of the expectation that I could do it all, and instead doing less but with more heart and awareness.

One regular Wednesday during a heart-to-heart one-on-one with one of my team members, I shared my recent discovery.

'Creating space is about intention,' I said tucking my legs under my desk to face the heater.

'Like carving out time for yourself?' Laura asked, her spoon swirling silently in her cup.

'Exactly,' I nodded, recalling how I'd started setting digital boundaries like no screens in the morning or before bed to give myself that precious time to breathe and reflect without distractions creeping in.

I have regular one-on-one meetings with my team where

we don't talk about work. We share experiences and talk about anything we like other than work, such as discussing rituals that help us, like taking five mindful breaths before picking up our phones or sipping tea without distraction starting work. These aren't grand spiritual overhauls. They are micro-revolutions.

'Gratitude breathing' became another favourite exercise for me, which involved a moment when we named three things we were grateful for with each breath we took together during our meetups.

The simple act of walking barefoot on grass was another favourite. It ignited memories from my childhood. These barefoot adventures through backyards or parks were grounding moments when stress threatened to overwhelm me. It always brought me back to the present.

Mindfulness in the everyday

I stopped searching for 'perfect' balance and instead sought presence in everyday moments:

- A mindful sip of tea in the backyard every morning before work.
- A one-minute eye lock with my own reflection in the mirror.
- Setting a timer to pause, breathe and scan my body for tension.
- Watching the sky change colours without trying to photograph it. Sometimes photographing it too, but not always...

These moments added up. They didn't erase my stress but they anchored me. They reminded me that I was here and not living my life on autopilot.

There was a quiet liberation in those pauses. A soft defiance against a culture that glorifies busyness or hustle culture and burnout.

Now I walk more slowly. I eat more consciously. I listen more deeply. And in doing so I've reclaimed something I didn't even realise I had lost… myself.

Let this be your invitation. Not to do more. But to be more present. In your morning. In your grief. In your joy. In your breath.

Because happiness isn't hidden in the noise. It's waiting quietly in the spaces you create.

PRACTICAL EXERCISES FOR CREATING MINDFUL SPACE IN A NOISY WORLD

If you feel like life is running away from you, I invite you to try these gentle practices to bring yourself back home.

1. Bookend your day with stillness

Start and end each day with five minutes of intentional silence. No phone. No to-do lists. Just you and your breath.

2. Grounding walks

Take short and slow walks, barefoot if possible. Focus on the feeling of the ground beneath you. Use each step as a reminder to be where you are.

3. Gratitude breathing

Inhale slowly. With each breath, name one thing you're grateful for. Do this three times. Feel how it shifts your energy.

Breath 1 – Grateful for:

Breath 2 – Grateful for:

Breath 3 – Grateful for:

4. Screen-free mornings

Resist the urge to reach for your phone. Instead, drink your coffee or tea while looking out the window. Journal. Stretch. Let your body arrive before your mind does.

5. One-minute eye contact

Stand before a mirror or sit with a loved one. Set a timer for 60 seconds. Make gentle eye contact. No words. Just presence. It's uncomfortable and profoundly healing.

ON A FINAL NOTE

What I've learned is this… mindfulness isn't a retreat from life, it's a return to it. It's noticing the space between your heartbeats. It's hearing your own breath and realising it's been speaking to you all along.

Balance doesn't come from mastering schedules. It comes from honouring your own rhythm. From noticing when you need to pause, reset and just be.

CHAPTER 15

Self-care and putting your needs first

BEFORE I BEGAN my journey towards mindfulness, my calendar was a patchwork quilt of other people's needs filled with meetings, birthdays, weddings, family catch-ups, late-night work calls, dinners with friends… events I didn't have the energy to attend but did anyway. I was the dependable one. The overachiever. The one who showed up no matter what was unravelling inside.

I always thought love was service. That kindness was synonymous with self-sacrifice. And so I gave my time, energy, space and presence until there was barely a whisper left of myself.

It was an overcast Saturday morning. I had barely slept, my mind cluttered with overdue reports and unreturned texts. I remember sitting on the edge of the bed with my body aching in a way that had nothing to do with illness and everything to do with depletion. I blinked at the clock and felt the slow and sinking dread of another day that wasn't mine as I had to attend someone's baby shower. A silent sob rose from my chest as I whispered to myself, '*I can't do this anymore*'.

That moment wasn't my lowest but it was my most honest. And it was yet another moment that changed my life.

The myth of selflessness

Growing up I was always praised for being 'the good girl.' I was the elder one, the more responsible sibling. I learned early that pleasing others earned approval. That saying 'yes' made me valuable. But nobody told me that overextending myself would someday cost me my peace, health and happiness.

I believed that saying no meant letting someone down.

That rest was laziness.

That putting myself first was selfish.

But burnout isn't noble. It's not a badge of honour; it's a warning light on the dashboard of your soul. And when we ignore it long enough it forces a reckoning.

Mine came in the form of tears over a sink full of dishes and a to-do list I couldn't face. I was terrified that if I stopped everything would fall apart.

The truth? The only thing falling apart was me.

Reclaiming my time

It started with a Tuesday. A single, radical, life-saving Tuesday.

I called in sick to work, not for a fever or a migraine but for exhaustion. Not just the kind that sleep cures but the soul-deep weariness that demands stillness. I lay on the couch with a book I didn't read, and tea beside me that I didn't drink. For hours, guilt paced like a nervous cat around my mind. But I didn't move. I stayed with the discomfort. I let myself be.

And somewhere between 11:00 am and 3:00 pm, a quiet truth dawned:

The world doesn't crumble when I take time out to rest. But I might if I don't.

That day became a beginning. Not a grand overhaul but a series of micro-rebellions in favour of myself.

Building my self-care compass

With time I realised self-care wasn't face masks and spa days, though those have their own place. It was boundaries, intentionality and listening to my own breath again.

My partner and I began what we called the Self-Care Compass: a check-in tool that helped us stay grounded in our needs each day.

We asked ourselves four questions:

- Physical: Did I nourish my body with movement, rest or good food?
- Emotional: Did I acknowledge how I truly felt today?
- Mental: What thoughts did I believe and were they kind?
- Spiritual: Did I do anything that made me feel connected to something greater: music, time in nature, prayer, presence?

Some days just answering those questions reminded me that I still mattered.

We also created a personalised Self-Care Menu, a list of small but manageable actions we could reach for on hard days:

- Take a beach walk.
- Say no to one non-essential social obligation.
- Drink a full glass of water.
- Watch an old favourite movie.

- Write one truth I'm proud of.
- Call someone who lifts me up.

It wasn't revolutionary. But it was consistent. And that changed everything.

The sacred 'no'

As I described in Chapter 9: The importance of boundaries and saying no, learning to say no was one of my most powerful transformations.

I started small, by declining a Zoom call I didn't have energy for, and letting a birthday text suffice instead of dragging myself to a gathering I didn't want to attend. Slowly I reclaimed time that was mine without any apology.

I even practised saying no in front of mirrors and laughing through my awkwardness.

'No, that doesn't work for me right now.'

'No, I'm prioritising rest today.'

'No, but thank you for thinking of me.'

Each time my voice grew steadier. Each 'no' was a yes to myself.

The 'Me Time' Ritual

Eventually I carved out what I now call my 'Me Time'. It's a protected window of time once a week where no one else's needs are allowed. No work, no family obligations, no phone calls. Just me. A bath, a book, a nap, a movie, a dance around the living room, whatever feels nourishing.

'Me Time' became sacred for me.

Because it reminded me that I am not a machine. I am a person. And I deserve care without justification.

Self-care as a revolution

Self-care is not a luxury. It's not a reward for burning out. It's the foundation of health, happiness and meaningful relationships.

When we show up for ourselves first, we teach others how to show up for us too. We dismantle the system that glorifies martyrdom. We model what it looks like to rest without guilt, especially for kids and younger family members. To love ourselves enough to pause. To say enough before we hit rock bottom.

In doing so we don't just survive, we bloom.

PRACTICAL EXERCISES FOR YOUR SELF-CARE

If you're reading this and it resonates, here are three powerful ways to begin your own self-care journey.

1. The Daily Self-Care Compass

Each evening, reflect using the following:

Physical: Did I care for my body today?

Emotional: What feelings did I experience, and did I acknowledge them?

Mental: Were my thoughts kind or critical?

Spiritual: Did anything feel meaningful today?

Write it down. Let it guide your adjustments tomorrow.

2. Create your own Self-Care Menu

List 10 activities that calm or energise you. Keep it simple and accessible. Post it somewhere visible like on the fridge, your desk or phone lock screen.

Some ideas:

Water a plant.

Watch a favourite TV episode.

Lie down and listen to calming music.

Stretch for 10 minutes.

Unfollow one toxic social media account.

1. ____

2. ____

3. ____

4. ____

5. ____

6. ____

7. ____

8. ____

9. ____

10. ____

3. Practise the sacred 'no'

Even though we talked about saying 'no' in Chapter 9, it's so important I want to reiterate it here by offering this exercise.

Make a list of three commitments you often say 'yes' to out of guilt or habit. Write a kind way to say 'no' to each one. Practise out loud until it feels empowering.

Examples:

'I'm not available this weekend, but I hope it goes wonderfully.'

'I'd love to help, but I need to rest tonight.'

'I'm focusing on other priorities right now, thank you for understanding.'

Commitment 1:

How I will say 'no':

Commitment 2:

How I will say 'no':

____

____

Commitment 3:

____

____

How I will say 'no':

____

____

ON A FINAL NOTE

What would your life look like if your needs mattered as much as everyone else's?

Start there. Not from burnout but from worthiness.

Because the most radical thing you can do for your happiness, health and well-being is this:

Put yourself back at the centre of your own life.

And from that place, watch everything in your life bloom.

PART 6

HAPPINESS THROUGH RESILIENCE AND GROWTH

CHAPTER 16

From setbacks to strength

THE DAY I left my marriage, the skies mirrored the storm inside me… grey, low and heavy with rain. I sat parked in the driveway, engine off, hands frozen on the steering wheel, staring at the house that had held my dreams and my undoing. The same windows I once adorned with fairy lights for Diwali and Christmas now looked back at me like hollow eyes, indifferent and familiar all at once. I had decorated that home with memories, filling its rooms with love and laughter, but beneath the paint and plaster was a loneliness that had gone unspoken for a long time.

Inside the house, he was still asleep or pretending to be. I had timed my exit like a quiet heist, early, silent, without warning. My bags had been packed for days, stashed carefully in the boot of my car under the cover of night while my heart thundered with fear. The sound of my own breathing felt deafening in the stillness. I half-expected the porch light to flick on and for someone to call out and stop me. No one did.

What people rarely speak about is the shame of leaving. Not just the fear, though fear was there in spades, but the shame that clings to you like a second skin. The shame of breaking something you swore to protect. The shame of walking away from a version of life you once begged the universe to grant you. It felt like failing a secret test, one everyone else seemed to pass but me.

The truth? I had already been leaving him, piece by piece, emotionally and spiritually for years. It happened gradually. Death by a thousand quiet cuts. Each dismissive comment, each moment of belittling disguised as 'just joking' and each time I bit my tongue for the sake of peace caused me to lose parts of myself. By the end I had become translucent. I moved through that house like a shadow. Seen, but not felt.

That morning wasn't the last time I left. Like many women caught in the undertow of familiarity, I went back twice. Apologies, promises, tears, rings taken off and put back on again. But something had shifted. The version of me that once stayed out of duty had begun to unravel. And eventually, she couldn't be stitched back together.

That first departure was not the end. But it was the beginning of it.

Falling apart in plain sight

When I finally left for good, it didn't feel like a triumphant escape; it felt like an amputation. I moved into a shared apartment with strangers. The room smelled of detergent and fresh paint, clean but unfamiliar. My mother flew in to help with the move, her presence a fragile lifeline. She made me tea that first night, lemon and ginger, and handed me a pink mug that read 'You've Got This' in bubbly font. I wanted to hurl it across the room.

'You're doing the right thing,' she said gently tucking a

blanket around my shoulders. I nodded but the words lodged in my throat like stones.

When night fell, when the world was quiet and the distractions faded away, the grief poured in like a deluge. I would curl up in the corner of that unfamiliar bed, my head buried in a pillow, and I would cry until the hollow space inside me ached with exhaustion. These weren't refined tears; they were uncontrolled, animal sounds that gasped for breath.

It wasn't just the end of a marriage I was mourning. It was the collapse of the identity I had spent years building. The good wife. The peacekeeper. The perfectionist. The one who made it work no matter what. I had laughed at family jokes that were hurtful. Smiled through holidays that felt empty. Smoothed conflict like one irons a tablecloth before guests arrive, ensuring everything is neat and acceptable.

Now that mask was gone and so was the person I had been beneath it.

Who was I without that role? What did it mean to be just... me?

The quiet rebuilding

There was no cinematic moment of awakening or change for me. No dramatic sunrise run or a yoga retreat in Ubud. My return to self was painfully quiet. It happened in ordinary ways, like changing the bedsheets after a crying spell, deleting his number from my favourites and completely from my phone, and learning to cook a meal without bursting into tears from muscle memory.

One morning after my mum returned overseas following her help with my move, I forced myself to go for a walk around the block. I had to physically force my legs to move. The sunlight felt too harsh. My eyes stung from lack of sleep, but I moved. And that was something. A woman pushing a stroller passed by me and offered a soft smile. A man walking his dog nodded as we crossed paths. That brief moment of being seen, not as a wife, a daughter or a victim but simply as a person, cracked something open inside me. I returned home and cried, not from despair, but from the quiet shock of still existing.

Another time I unpacked the last of my boxes and hung up my dresses in the new wardrobe. For weeks, I had lived out of suitcases, still unsure if I belonged in this new life. But hanging my clothes, choosing hangers, spacing them out, felt symbolic. Like maybe I wasn't just visiting and in survival mode anymore. Maybe I planned to stay.

One evening a friend asked me, 'What does emotional safety mean to you now?'

I had no answer. I had spent so long tolerating the intolerable that the concept of emotional safety felt foreign. I didn't even know how to recognise it, let alone expect it.

So I began small. I built new rituals. I started journalling each morning, pouring whatever was on my mind onto the page… grief, rage, boredom, hunger, gratitude. It all belonged. I made lists:

Things I was proud of.

Things I wanted to learn & do.

Things I'd forgotten I loved.

One day I wrote: 'I used to dance. I miss her.'

So on a whim, I signed up for a beginner's pole dancing class. I went alone, anxious, my heart pounding in my ears.

I wore old gym tights and borrowed courage. I was terrible. I fell. I bruised. But I smiled, really smiled for the first time in months.

That night I cried again. Not because I was broken. But because for the first time, I felt alive again.

The turning point

The moment everything shifted didn't look like a breakthrough for me either. It was a grey Saturday afternoon. I was home alone, drinking lukewarm tea, wrapped in a cardigan three sizes too big. Rain tapped on the windows. I was scrolling through social media and saw a quote:

'Setbacks don't break me. They shape me.'

It stopped me cold. I read it again. Then again. I wrote it down in my journal. I underlined it. I circled it. It wasn't just a sentence. It was a stake in the ground.

That mantra became my compass.

I began to see every heartbreak not as a weakness but as a forge. A fire that melted the illusions of who I thought I had to be and shaped the truth of who I actually was.

Resilience, brick by brick

Resilience wasn't something I stumbled upon one day. It didn't come wrapped in a TED Talk or handed to me in a therapist's office. I built it. Brick by brick. Breath by breath. One shaky step after another.

It showed up in ordinary things:

- Cooking a homemade dinner instead of ordering something to numb myself

- Sitting in silence without Netflix, scrolling or drinking wine
- Creating a budget, tracking expenses, facing the financial chaos I had avoided for months
- Sleeping… really sleeping through the night, undisturbed by nightmares or memories.

I began to surround myself with people who didn't just support me, they saw me. My friend, let's call her Ivy, sent me voice notes every morning for weeks, 'You are stronger than you feel today.' My mum mailed me booties she knitted with a note that said, 'For all the cold days ahead you're going to conquer.'

And then there was me.

The version of me who had been silent for too long. The girl who used to dance barefoot in her bedroom, who had big dreams and a bold laugh. She was coming back. Slowly and fiercely.

The woman I am today

I haven't gone into all the details here, not yet. Some parts of my story are still healing. But here's what I can tell you with certainty. That journey with the pain, the loss, the loneliness, it shaped me into who I am today.

I am not the woman I was before I broke. I am stronger. Wiser. Softer in all the right places and steel in others.

If I could go back, I wouldn't change a thing. Not the heartbreak. Not the mistakes. Not the years of trying to make something unworkable work. Because all of it, all the setbacks, the stumbles, the silence, it made me into the woman I am today.

And that woman? She knows her worth. She knows her

voice. And she knows that resilience isn't the absence of struggle. It's the decision to rise, again and again, no matter how many times you've fallen.

This is not the end

People often ask me now, 'How did you find happiness again?' And the truth is… I didn't find it. I built it, everyday.

One difficult, beautiful, ordinary day at a time.

I still have days when I feel tender. But now I know tenderness isn't weakness. It's evidence that I've lived, that I've loved and that I'm still healing and learning.

So if you are reading this and wondering whether you'll ever feel whole again, please know: you don't have to leap. Just take the next right step. Then another. And another.

That's how strength is born.

And happiness? It's not at the finish line. It's in the rebuilding. In the resilience. It's in you.

PRACTICAL EXERCISES TO BUILD YOUR STRENGTH

The exercises here are not just exercises, they're invitations to reconnect with your power, your joy and your inner resilience.

1. Resilience timeline

Create a timeline of your life's major setbacks. Under each one, write what you survived and beside it, note what it taught you. You'll begin to see that your strength is not theoretical, it's proven.

Example:

- 2012 – Job loss → Learned how to rebuild with new skills
- 2014 – Divorce → Reclaimed personal freedom and voice

Use this space to write your own:

2. The identity reclamation list

List all the roles you've played (e.g. caregiver, spouse, achiever). Then write a new list: Who are you beyond those roles? (e.g. creative soul, loyal friend, dancer, healer). Who do you want to reclaim?

Prompt:

- Former roles: mother, partner, manager
- True identity: writer, explorer, survivor, artist

Use this space to write your own:

3. Write a letter to your past self

Pick a version of you that endured pain. Write them a letter, not with blame but with compassion. Tell them what you know now, and what they did right, even when it didn't feel like enough.

Start with:

'Dear younger me, I know you were trying your best...'

---

4. The Three Anchors

Identify three people (past or present) who remind you of your strength. Keep their names on a notecard. When you feel lost, ask yourself: What would they tell me now?

Example:

- Grandma Rose: 'You always get back up.'
- My best friend James: 'You are more powerful than your circumstances.'

Write your own:

Anchor No. 1:

Anchor No. 2:

____

Anchor No. 3:

____

5. Joy sparks

Make a list of 20 small things that make you feel joy (a scent, a song, a walk, a memory). When you feel overwhelmed, pick one. Joy isn't the end of healing, it's part of the process.

Example:

- Fresh linen
- The smell of jasmine
- Dancing in the kitchen
- A warm shower
- Watching sunrise

Write your own:

1. ____

2. ____

3. ____

4. ____

5. ____

6. ____

7. _______________________________________

8. _______________________________________

9. _______________________________________

10. ______________________________________

11. ______________________________________

12. ______________________________________

13. ______________________________________

14. ______________________________________

15. ______________________________________

16. ______________________________________

17. ______________________________________

18. ______________________________________

19. ______________________________________

20. ______________________________________

ON A FINAL NOTE

If you are standing in the ruins of what once felt like everything, if the weight of your choices or your circumstances feels too heavy to hold, please know this: you are not alone, you are not broken, and this moment does not define you.

Our setbacks are not roadblocks, they are redirections. Sometimes they tear down the illusions we build our lives around so something better, truer and more aligned with us can take shape. These life moments force us to remember who we are and return home to those parts we silenced or lost along the way in order to survive our circumstances.

Resilience isn't loud. Sometimes it's as quiet as getting out of bed when you don't feel like it. As gentle as making yourself a cup of coffee or as fierce as saying, *'This is not how my story ends...'*

CHAPTER 17

Embracing change and transformation

'Sometimes the bravest thing you can do is start over.'

A FEW YEARS ago when I was living in Sydney, I had finally landed a job that on paper was everything I had ever worked for. A sleek modern office perched high in a skyscraper above the city skyline. A title that made a buzz at industry mixers. An ensemble of top minds in information technology consulting. I had arrived.

Or so I thought…

Each morning I'd step into a building lined with polished floors and ambitious chatter. The scent of coffee lingered around like fake comfort. Everyone in the office constantly rustled through meetings with performance decks in hand and well-crafted smiles. Success was a currency, and burnout was an unspoken toll in that organisation.

Behind closed doors the culture was cutthroat. People jostled for visibility and sabotaged each other for praise. Leaders managed not through inspiration but with scrutiny, measuring your worth in every hour billed, every email sent and every minute of availability. Growth sessions? Personal development? Admin tasks? Those were luxuries. 'Do it on your own time,' they'd say.

And I did. Until I couldn't anymore.

One Monday morning I caught my reflection in the frosted glass of my office door. The woman staring back wore a crisp blazer and red lipstick but the light in her eyes had vanished. I barely recognised myself. My soul, once vibrant and full of spark, had gone quiet.

That day I sat in yet another pointless meeting. Numb. Nodding. Disconnected. I walked out, got in my car and cried like a dam had burst. No music, no movement, just the sound of my breath shaking through sobs as I remembered that I had promised myself once that *I can't keep living like this.*

The quiet rebellion

That wasn't a breakdown but it was a beginning for me. I took some time off to clear my head, take a break and spend time with my family in India.

I was sitting with my mum when she asked, 'How's work going?' and I responded, 'It's not good. I feel like I'm trapped'. Mum responded with, 'Who is keeping you trapped?'

The answer was loud and clear for me. It was me. I was keeping myself trapped in this job that I hated.

Three weeks later I handed in my resignation. My voice trembled as I said the words aloud but something remarkable happened. Relief. Like fresh air after years of holding my breath. I wasn't falling, I was *freeing* myself.

I wasn't just leaving a job. I was shedding an identity that no longer fit. I was no longer willing to wear my burnout like a badge of honour. The prestige wasn't worth the anxiety attacks. The pay check couldn't pay for the parts of myself I had abandoned to earn it.

Some people thought I was brave to quit without having found a new job first, since it was coming into the holiday period where people would be on leave and the job market slowed down. Truthfully, I was terrified. But underneath the fear was something stronger: a tiny flicker of hope that maybe, just maybe, I could build a life that didn't require me to shrink to fit it.

The slow becoming

Transformation doesn't announce itself with a bang. It creeps in through cracked windows, whispering, 'What if?' It invites you to sit in discomfort, to unlearn, to unravel.

In the months that followed, I tried to rebuild myself.

Not with dramatic changes but with small, quiet choices.

- I learned to rest without guilt.
- I explored creativity without deadlines.
- I replaced performance with presence.

I painted for the first time since high school. The brush shook in my hand, but the colour reminded me I was still alive. I reconnected with old friends, not over achievements but over shared silence, old stories and coffee. I found joy in dog walks, baking banana bread and dancing barefoot in my living room.

Each of these moments felt insignificant on their own. But together they wove a new story, one where happiness wasn't a milestone but a way of living.

Lessons the journey taught me

Change isn't always chosen, but transformation is.

Life hands us changes we never asked for or foresaw, whether it's relationships dissolving, jobs shifting unexpectedly or a diagnosis we didn't see coming. Those moments can feel disorienting at best. However, how we respond shapes our reality more than any circumstance ever could. We can't control those moments. But transformation? That's ours to claim.

Starting over is not failure, but it's proof of courage and wisdom.

We like to speak of reinvention as though it were this effortless and glamorous thing, but the reality is far more complex; it's raw, unsettling and profoundly difficult. True reinvention takes a kind of courage that not many possess. Having the courage to release what no longer serves you, whether a toxic relationship, a dull friendship or a stagnant career, is brave but necessary. Each time we find the courage to confront the truth and choose change, we make a powerful declaration of our capability for growth and resilience.

Breakdowns have the seeds of breakthroughs in them.

Those ugly moments that undo us, the ones where we believe we won't make it through, are frequently the ones that reconstruct us stronger, truer and more whole.

At some point in this chapter, I realised I wasn't just writing about my own transformation; I was writing to you, my dear reader. So I penned a letter addressed to you, to provide an open space for embracing your own transformations.

Dear you,

There will come a day when you realise you are holding on to something… maybe a relationship, an old friendship, a career or a version of yourself that no longer serves you. And fear will whisper all the reasons you should stay.

But here's the reality… letting go isn't the end of your book. It's the invitation to write the next chapter.

It's time to let go of what no longer serves you, to move towards dreams postponed or potential unexplored, even when fear tugs at your heartstrings. Trust that releasing old patterns creates space for new beginnings.

I want you to know that you are allowed to pivot, to restart, to leave and reinvent. You are allowed to be both terrified and brave. You are allowed to choose yourself.

With love,

Someone who has been where you are.

The quiet bravery of starting again

Transformation does not happen in one big leap. Transformation is in a hundred small steps and most of them will be uncomfortable and unclear.

But every step matters. Every time you choose honesty over pretension, courage over comfort, trust over fear, you're building the bridge to your next life.

And when you eventually cross, you'll see that beginning again doesn't include becoming someone else. It means at last becoming someone true.

Change as I've learned is not always chosen. But transformation, that's the part we own.

We don't always get to pick the storm, but we do get to build the boat.

Here's what I now know:

You don't need to be fearless to begin again.
You just need to be willing.

PRACTICAL EXERCISES FOR
YOUR TRANSFORMATION

1. Transformation timeline

Draw a timeline of your life. Mark the *unexpected turns* like job losses, breakups, relocations, illnesses, new beginnings.

Under each point, write:

- What was lost?
- What was gained?
- How did I grow?

You'll begin to see you've *survived yourself into wisdom*. Use the space below to map your journey:

2. The bridge practice

Visualise your current life as one riverbank. Familiar. Predictable. But stifling.

On the other side is your *next version*: free, radiant, aligned.

Ask yourself:

- What fears am I carrying that weigh me down?
- What can I leave behind to lighten the crossing?
- What strengths am I bringing with me?

Now take one symbolic action like a phone call, a walk, a journal entry, to begin that crossing.

Reflection space:

3. Write a letter to the you who stayed too long

Write a compassionate letter to the version of you who stayed in a place that dimmed your light. Not to blame, but to honour her resilience.

Tell her:

- What she did right.
- What you now understand.
- That it's safe to move forward.

Your letter:

4. Permission slips

Write yourself permission slips for:

- Saying no without guilt.
- Starting again at any age.
- Choosing joy over duty.
- Resting before you're exhausted.

Stick them on your mirror. Carry one in your wallet. Let them become your new rules for living.

Create your permission slips below:

5. Mantras for reinvention

Let these words carry you through uncertainty:

- 'I am allowed to change.'
- 'I am more than what I've endured.'
- 'The unknown is where my magic lives.'
- 'Peace is my new measure of success.'

Repeat them daily. Write them. Whisper them. Believe them.

ON A FINAL NOTE

We often resist change because we fear losing who we are. But what if we're not losing ourselves, just outgrowing who we were *never meant to continue being*?

Transformation isn't neat. It's messy and miraculous. It will break you open and show you what you're made of.

So if you're standing at a threshold today uncertain, afraid, curious, please know this:

You are not behind.

You are not broken.

You are simply becoming.

And that… is a beautiful thing.

PART 7

SUSTAINING YOUR HAPPINESS

CHAPTER 18

Loving your own company

FOR MOST OF my life, solitude felt like a frenemy… a strange, lingering presence I couldn't quite welcome or banish. Growing up, I associated being alone with failure and not being chosen. In my twenties, I filled every spare moment with noise, crowded brunches, overbooked calendars and relationships that were more placeholders than true connections. Silence was something I ran from.

But nothing forced me to confront my relationship with solitude more than my marriage and its painful unravelling.

The marriage that silenced me

During my marriage, silence was a weapon. There were days when my ex-husband's cold shoulders and punishing quiet would stretch for hours, sometimes days. I used to think I was being strong, believing that enduring the tension without complaint was proof of my resilience. But the truth was more complicated: I was shrinking, moulding myself into whatever shape I thought would keep the peace.

The house we shared wasn't filled with warmth, even when

it was bustling with noise. There was always an undercurrent, a quiet threat that made me feel as if I were constantly walking on thin ice. And somehow, in the midst of all that tension, I started to lose the sound of my own voice and my sense of self.

When the marriage finally crumbled, the house I shared with strangers felt like an empty cavern. The echoes of those silences still clung to the walls. I thought I'd been prepared for freedom but the quiet was deafening.

Running from the stillness

In the months following the divorce, I moved into a new apartment by myself. But to ensure I was never alone, I threw myself into life with frantic energy. I signed up for every gym class, said yes to every brunch invite and kept my calendar so full there was barely a sliver of white space. My phone was my lifeline: group chats, dating apps, endless notifications. I was determined not to let the silence swallow me again.

It worked for a while. The buzz of social existence dulled the hurt. There were weeks when I barely spent a single evening alone, switching between dinner parties, after-work happy hours and weekends with friends.

But then something odd happened.

I started to get confused and felt lonely in rooms with lots of people.

I would be sitting at a long dinner table, conversation buzzing around me and suddenly I would feel a hollow tug in my chest as if I didn't belong there. I'd smile, nod and laugh at the right moments but inside I felt invisible and disconnected. Surrounded but unseen.

It dawned on me one evening, as I left yet another crowded gathering, that I felt lonelier in those rooms than I did in my own living room. Being 'on' all the time and performing happiness, while keeping the mask intact was exhausting.

Choosing solitude, slowly

So I started saying no. At first it was just occasionally. A dinner party skipped here, a weekend plan politely declined there. Then more often. Friends noticed: 'You've been quiet lately,' or 'You have to come to the party, I won't take no for an answer' they'd say. But I wasn't withdrawing out of sadness anymore. I was creating space for myself.

At home, in that once empty feeling apartment, I began to experiment with being alone not as punishment but as a choice.

One rainy Saturday morning stands out. I sat by the window with tea steaming in my hands and instead of reaching for my phone to fill the void, I let the silence settle. I found an old journal that had been tucked away since my marriage and began to write. Its journalling I have realised that through my life has brought me out of difficult emotional times and reminded me who I am; and even though I keep forgetting about it when life happens, it's something I always come back to like a home.

What spilled out surprised me. Not pain, not entirely, but dreams. Forgotten ones. Ideas I had shelved for years. Paintings I'd once wanted to create. Books I'd wanted to read. Places I'd wanted to see. Words I'd wanted to write.

It was like meeting myself for the first time in years.

The shift from loneliness to solitude

The truth no one ever tells you is that loneliness and solitude are not synonyms. Loneliness is an ache, a feeling of absence, a hollow space shaped like the people who aren't there. Solitude, on the other hand, is a presence; it's a room you fill with yourself.

That shift didn't happen overnight. At first being alone meant sitting uncomfortably and staring at thoughts I'd pushed away for far too long. But over time, being alone no longer felt like abandonment; it started feeling like authenticity.

I realised that being home with myself felt more honest than sitting at yet another crowded table where I felt like I had to smile through the dissonance.

There is liberation in that moment, the one where you realise you are not waiting for someone to save you from yourself. You already have what you need.

And in that quiet space, something profound happened; I reminded myself that I needed to focus on myself: I began auditing all the relationships in my life

I noticed which relationships drained me and which ones gave me life, which friendships were based on convenience and which were based on care and connection. Slowly, I started to release the ones that no longer fit, that I had been clinging to out of habit, fear of being alone or the desire to hold on to an old version of myself.

As I made myself scarce in those old circles, I began to fill my life differently, not with noise but with meaning.

I started making space and time for things I enjoyed doing like reading, writing or just sitting still and enjoying my own company. And what I realised is that I loved my own company, sometimes a little too much.

PRACTICAL EXERCISES FOR LEARNING TO LOVE YOUR OWN COMPANY

These are the practices that helped me not just find happiness in my own presence but keep it alive. Perhaps you can try them too.

1. Solo date

I started taking myself out on purpose. At first it felt awkward: a breakfast for one, a seat in the back row of a movie theatre or wandering an art gallery alone. But something shifted when I stopped apologising for my presence. Now solo dates are my favourite dates. Try it. Take yourself somewhere not as a consolation prize but as a celebration.

2. Mirror practice

There was a time in my life where mirrors felt like enemies. They reflected a woman who'd dimmed herself to survive or someone who was not enough. After my divorce, I forced myself to face her again. Each morning I stood in front of the mirror and said one kind thing aloud, even when I didn't believe it. Someone once said to me while giving me some work advice that you have to 'fake it till you make it' to succeed and it stuck with me, so I said words that I did not even believe to myself like:

'I am enough.'

'I am learning.'

'I am still here, I'm growing.'

And over time, the voice softened. Over time I believed myself. Try it, and you might too.

3. Alone-time audit

Ask yourself and write down your responses to these prompts below:

- Do I avoid being alone? Why?
- When I'm alone, what activities make me feel most alive?
- What can I let go of, plans, people, patterns to create more sacred solo moments?

Your answers might surprise you. Mine surely did. And I repeat these exercises regularly because as humans we conveniently forget to do things that are hard (for our emotions).

Use the space to write yours:

4. Finding comfort in silence

In the early days, silence triggered old fears, but I learned to soften into it. Five deep breaths. A slow cup of tea. A quiet barefoot beach walk without headphones just to enjoy the feeling of sand in my feet. These tiny rituals trained my body to see stillness not as threat but as sanctuary.

Create a list of your own that you can go back to every time you feel fear or doubt shadowing you.

-
-
-
-
-
-
-
-
-
-
-
-
-

ON A FINAL NOTE

There will still be days when I crave connection, when I need someone to share the joke or the sunset with. But now I no longer fear my own company.

Because of what I discovered sitting by that rain-streaked window is that happiness isn't something someone else hands you. It's something you learn to create and to keep alive, in the quietest of rooms with no one there but you.

And that, perhaps, is the greatest freedom of all.

Remember: Loving your own company is a journey. Use these templates as often as you need to rediscover who you are beneath the noise.

CHAPTER 19

Mindset of creating abundance

SCARCITY WAS THE language of my childhood.

It wasn't that we didn't have enough – we did. My parents both held respectable jobs, our pantry was never bare, my school shoes were always polished, and we had regular family vacations. But there was an unspoken tension in the air, a constant undercurrent of 'hold on tight because it could all slip away' in a split second.

I remember clutching a single bill in my small hand, my dad's voice in my ear: 'Save it. You never know when you might need it later.' His words were born from his own history and stories of parents who lost everything in the war, of lives rebuilt from rubble and broken dreams. They carried that fear like a family heirloom and without even realising it, they passed it to me.

My grandmother Moni-Mumma, as I called her with love, lived with us and took care of me and my brother while our parents were working. She was a big influence in our lives in term of shaping our little baby brains towards the world. She would often sit me down on humid summer evenings in the front yard and tell me stories from her childhood, stories that were both mesmerising and haunting. She spoke of the days before the India–Pakistan Partition when her family lived in Sindh, a region that is now part of Pakistan. They were wealthy then, owning land, a sprawling ancestral home and businesses that thrived. But all of that crumbled in 1947 when the Partition split the country along religious lines. Hindus, Muslims and Sikhs who had lived as neighbours for generations suddenly found themselves divided by fear, politics and violence.

The Partition of India was one of the largest and most agonising mass migrations in history. When British India was divided into two independent nations, India and Pakistan, millions of individuals were forced to leave their homes overnight. My grandparents' families were Hindu and had been ordered to leave or lose their lives. They were thrown out of their own home, watching strangers move in as they fled with only the clothes on their backs and a few belongings clutched to their chests. My grandmother described the chaos, the long, perilous journeys on overcrowded trains, the sound of weeping that seemed endless, the constant fear of being killed before crossing the border, living in refugee camps and the silent resilience of those who lost everything but kept moving.

Even decades later, those memories lived in her like unhealed scars. The fear of losing it all again seeped into her parenting, into her conversations, into the way she handled even the smallest things like how she would fold away sheets of newspaper to reuse, or how she'd admonish us not to waste food, reminding us softly, 'You don't know what it's like to have nothing.' Those stories weren't just history lessons, they were the roots of the scarcity mindset I inherited without even knowing it.

It wasn't about the money, though. Scarcity invaded other

areas of my life too, such as time, love and joy. I starved my dreams, not wanting to use up too much, fearing the well would run dry. I overanalysed friendships, wondering if I was bringing enough value to the table or if I was simply taking up space. I lived life as if joy were something delicate, something that would break if I held on too tightly.

A watershed moment for me

Years later, I attended a small community fundraiser one evening. It wasn't fancy; just a few tables filled with homemade cake, hand-painted pottery and used books. In one corner, a local artist stood beside a group of her paintings, each one bright and cheerful.

She spoke of her work with passion, warmth and openness in her voice. She told stories of the strokes of the brush and how one painting emerged from the colour of the sea after a storm, while another was conceived after a night spent tossing and turning in heartbreak. And then she said something that pierced through me:

'I don't worry if they all sell. Sharing them is enough.'

Her joy wasn't tied to outcome. She wasn't clutching her art the way I'd spent my life clutching everything that felt scarce. She was giving, freely and joyfully, and in that giving she seemed fuller, not emptied.

That night was a turning point for me.

I began to see that abundance isn't just about money. It isn't even just about 'having enough.' It's a mindset. A way of walking through life believing there is more everywhere, more love, more opportunity, more beauty than we could ever possibly hold.

One day soon after, I was staring at an empty vase inside

the cupboard when something shifted within me. I went to the shops and bought some flowers. I didn't buy them for anyone else; I didn't wait for someone to buy them for me. That single act was a rebellion against scarcity. That vase became my reminder that abundance doesn't wait for permission; it's something we create.

Letting go of scarcity mindset

But the generations and years of scarcity thinking don't dissolve in a single epiphany.

At first I tried to 'think abundantly', the way you might put on a new coat awkwardly and self-consciously, hoping no one notices it doesn't quite fit yet. I started saying yes to things I might have turned down before like a challenging project at work, a weekend away with friends, because, for the first time, I wasn't focused on what I might lose. Instead, I began to ask, 'What might I gain?'

And here's what surprised me the most: the more I leaned into that question, the more life leaned back.

Opportunities appeared where before there had only been walls. Setbacks became lessons instead of verdicts. I stopped clutching so tightly to every coin, every hour, every relationship, and something miraculous happened: space opened up for more.

More opportunities opened up for work, more money in my bank accounts despite spending more, more real conversations and friendships, and more love and joy in my life.

The truth about abundance

What I have learned is that abundance is not what you have in your hands; it's what you allow to flow through them. It's in my grandmother's tales shared over generations that I am reminded that even with unimaginable losses, our lives can be rebuilt. It's in the kindness of strangers making space without asking on a crowded bus so you can sit; the affection of shared meals with loved ones and friends; and the resilience to believe that there is enough happiness, love and opportunity for all of us. And it's in the quiet moments and generous acts I witness every day, the moments that show abundance isn't just a concept in books; it's a way of life.

When we transition from grasping to releasing, from fear to faith, we discover that joy is not something we have to chase; it is something we can nurture, sustain and share. And the beautiful truth is this: the more we practise abundance, the more it grows, spilling into every corner of our lives and into the lives of those around us.

It's about knowing that giving doesn't diminish you; it multiplies you.

When you buy coffee for the stranger behind you in the queue (try it), you don't just make their day; you remind yourself that generosity is a renewable resource. By complimenting another person sincerely, you not only brighten their moment, you also expand your own capacity for joy.

Scarcity whispers, 'Hold on.'

Abundance says, 'Let it flow.'

Living in the flow

There's a lightness that comes when you stop gripping everything so tightly.

You start to see the world differently. You trust that what you give will return, not always in the same form but in ways that are often more beautiful than you imagined.

Abundance isn't a bank balance. It's a breath. It's the decision to open your hands, open your heart and let life move through you instead of clutching it to pieces.

When you adopt an abundance mindset, happiness stops being something you chase and becomes something you keep alive.

Because abundance, once invited, doesn't just stay, it grows.

PRACTICAL EXERCISES FOR CREATING AN ABUNDANCE MINDSET

Use this space to reflect, write and practise shifting your mindset from scarcity to abundance. Each exercise has space for your thoughts, lists and reflections.

1. Abundance inventory

Set aside 20 minutes with a cup of tea or coffee and a quiet space. Write down everything you already have, not just possessions but moments, skills and relationships. This will help you see the wealth already present in your life.

What do I already have that brings me joy? (List below)

2. Gratitude as a daily practice

Keep a notebook by your bed. Every night, write down three things that brought you joy that day even if they're small: a warm breeze, a text from a friend, the smell of dinner cooking. Over time, gratitude rewires the brain and it trains your eyes to see abundance where scarcity once lived.

Start here today.

Today's gratitude list:

1. ____

2. ____

3. ____

3. Abundance affirmations

Words matter. Start your mornings by speaking abundance into your day. Say them out loud, even if you feel silly at first:

- Life supports me in every way.
- Opportunities are always finding me.
- I am open to receiving more.

Write your own affirmations here:

____

____

____

Affirmations are like seeds. Plant them daily and watch them grow.

4. The generosity experiment

For one week make a conscious choice to give every single day. It doesn't have to be money. Offer a smile, a compliment, a helping hand, an hour of your time. Notice how giving shifts the energy in your life and how much more comes back to you.

Daily acts of generosity:

Day 1: ____

Day 2: ____

Day 3: ____

Day 4: ____

Day 5: ____

Day 6: ____

Day 7: ____

ON A FINAL NOTE

Scarcity teaches you to survive, but abundance teaches you to live. Through the memories of my grandmother's resilience, my father's cautious wisdom and the gentle generous presence of my partner in my life, I have learned that abundance is not something we wait to earn, it's something we choose to believe in. It lives in our life stories, in our willingness to receive and make space for what's out there, and most of all in our capacity to give.

You don't need more to feel abundant. You just have to see your life differently. Every day you are offered a choice from the universe: to contract or expand, to fear or trust, to hold tight or let go.

So take a deep breath with me here. Open your hands and release the weight of 'I'm not enough' or 'I don't have enough' and step into the quiet, powerful trust that you already are enough. You already have enough. And there is more than enough to go around and share.

CHAPTER 20

Daily rituals for lifelong happiness

MOST OF MY life I chased happiness like a finish line, a white dot on the horizon that would appear after a graduation, a wedding, a promotion or a long-overdue vacation. I thought that joy would be wrapped in fireworks and trumpets and disperse the mundane ache of everyday days.

But it never did…

Instead I learned something quieter, almost whisper thin, a revelation that happiness never hides in those glittering milestones. It lies within the tiny and humble moments; the ones I'd been ignoring all those years. Happiness, as I discovered, lies more in the stitching we do in the fabric of our everyday lives and less in the grand acts or big milestones.

The morning ritual

The shift began after a particularly draining period of time at work, when life was a blur of deadlines and constant to-do lists. I remember waking up one morning, half asleep, already scrolling through messages and emails before I'd even risen.

My body was awake but my soul felt weighed down as if I'd been robbed of my own mornings.

I made a silent vow that day: I would not begin my day in disarray again.

The next morning, instead of reaching for my phone, I reached for a cup of tea. I brought it out into my backyard, where the dawn light had painted everything golden. I felt the cup in my hands as I sat still for the first time in years and listened to the birds chirping in the trees and the far-off hum of an awakening city.

I whispered a prayer to the quiet sky: 'Today, I choose patience.'

It felt awkward initially, similar to speaking with a stranger. But day by day, this ritual rooted itself. Some mornings, my intention was patience. Other mornings, it was courage, kindness or joy. The ritual wasn't about forcing a perfect day; it was about grounding myself before the whirlwind began.

And something remarkable happened: life slowed. Not on the outside; emails still came, deadlines still loomed, but inside, I wasn't rushing.

Evening gratitude ritual

Evenings were another matter entirely. For years, I ended my days mindlessly slumped on the couch, scrolling, TV providing background noise, numbing, avoiding the lingering sense of incompleteness.

Then one evening after journalling during a workshop exercise, I picked up an empty notebook and wrote down three things I was grateful for that day.

Over weeks, my journal filled with these tiny fragments of

joy, a mosaic of moments that proved life was softer, kinder and more abundant than my stressed-out brain wanted to admit.

As I have already described, gratitude became not just a practice but an anchor for me. Perhaps it can for you too.

Happiness is built daily

I used to think happiness was built in leaps: new jobs, big moves, bold decisions. Now I see it's built in layers like sediment in a riverbed, forming slowly through thousands of tiny deposits.

One of my most sacred rituals is what I call my 'Sunday Reset'. Every Sunday afternoon, I sit with a steaming cup of herbal tea and my notebook reflecting on the week that was.

I ask myself: What worked this week? What didn't?

It's not a self-criticism session; it's a soft inventory. Some weeks, I notice I laugh a lot. Others, I see I have overbooked myself, leaving little room to breathe. From these reflections, I adjust. I recalibrate. I heal.

These small rituals gave me something I didn't even know I was craving: a sense of agency. Life no longer just happened to me. I was choosing how to meet it.

How rituals saved me

After my marriage ended, when the silence became unbearable, I drowned myself in busyness: dinners, parties, endless coffee catch-ups, thinking that being constantly surrounded by people would heal me.

But as I've already described, the opposite happened. I began to feel lonelier in a crowded room than I did at home alone. The noise became exhausting.

So I started making myself scarce.

At first it was difficult to say no, but eventually evenings spent alone with my journal, mornings spent alone with my tea, and Sundays spent alone with my thoughts began to feel like acts of recovery.

I realised that happiness did not just lie in the finding of joy but in learning how to sustain it, how to cultivate it like a fragile fire. And that required space, silence and work on a daily basis.

PRACTICAL EXERCISES FOR
YOUR OWN DAILY JOY

This section is designed to help you create, track and sustain daily rituals that cultivate long-term happiness. Use these pages as a guide to develop meaningful habits, reflect on your journey and weave joy into your everyday life.

1. Joy menu

Create a list of 10 tiny, accessible rituals that bring you joy. They don't need to be grand, think a warm cup of tea before screens, five minutes of stretching before getting out of bed, a moment on your balcony breathing fresh air.

Pick three from your joy menu each day. Rotate them. Make them yours.

1. ____

2. ____

3. ____

4. ____

5. ____

6. ____

7. _______________________________

8. _______________________________

9. _______________________________

10. ______________________________

2. Morning mindset ritual

Each morning, jot down:

One intention: (e.g. I choose calm today.)

One gratitude: (e.g. I'm thankful for my health.)

One small joy goal: (e.g. I'll watch the sunset tonight.)

This takes five minutes. But it transforms the tone of your entire day.

Start here:

____

____

____

____

____

3. Midday reset

Set a 'joy alarm' on your phone. When it rings, stop for a micro-ritual: take a walk, listen to a favourite song or even just take three deep breaths. It's a reset button for your mind.

Describe your chosen ritual here:

Notes/reflections:

4. Evening gratitude practice

This is one we've talked about before, but I can't stress enough how a gratitude practice can change your life. So before you close your eyes, write down three things that made you smile today. Some days, they'll be monumental. Some days, they'll be as simple as the smell of rain or coffee. Both count.

Notes/reflections:

5. The weekly reset

On Sundays, spend 15 minutes reflecting:

What worked this week?

What drained me?

What small shifts can I make?

This keeps you aligned before you fall too far off course.

Notes/reflections:

ON A FINAL NOTE

These rituals are not about building a perfect life. They are about building a tended life, one where happiness isn't something you chase, but something you nurture, daily.

Happiness is not an accident. It's a practice.

When I look back now, it's not the milestones that shine brightest; it's the ordinary mornings with tea in my hands, quiet nights with my gratitude journal or just reading a good book before bed, and Sundays spent recalibrating.

Happiness doesn't live in someday. It lives in today, in the rituals we choose, again and again, until they become the quiet, steady rhythm of a life well-lived and a life well-loved.

CHAPTER 21

Sharing happiness and making a difference

I USED TO believe happiness was a deeply personal pursuit, a private little garden to tend, shielded from the chaos of the world. For years I thought that if I just worked harder on my own joy and if I journalled enough, meditated enough and healed enough, I would somehow arrive at this permanent state of contentment.

But life, in its quiet wisdom, had other plans.

It taught me, sometimes gently and sometimes like a sharp knock on the door at midnight, that happiness, when hoarded, withers. And when shared, it multiplies.

I didn't learn this from a book or a workshop or a glossy Instagram post. I learned it the day I met the man who would change the way I saw the world, not because he taught me but because he lived it.

After meeting my current partner, I began to gain a deeper understanding of sharing happiness. His effortless kindness and quiet generosity reshaped my perception of what it meant to make a difference. He didn't speak about it; he simply... lived it.

One ordinary afternoon, as we were leaving the grocery store with our arms heavy with bags and our minds already focused on dinner, we saw him. A homeless man sat cross-legged by the entrance, his head low and his voice barely audible as he asked for spare change.

People streamed past, with some averting their eyes. I felt an uncomfortable tug in my chest, the kind that whispers, 'Someone should do something', while your feet keep moving.

My partner paused, considering the man for a moment before stepping closer.

He crouched down and looked at the man. 'I don't have cash,' he whispered, 'but I can buy anything you wish from the shop.'

The man's head snapped up, shock tracing its way across his face. 'You're certain?' he asked, looking doubtful.

'Yeah mate, let's go,' my partner replied with a grin.

And so they walked back into the store together.

I lagged behind, half ashamed, half in wonder at my own hesitation.

Minutes later they emerged side by side, my partner grinning widely and the homeless man beaming back at him with a bag full of groceries.

There was no applause, no pat on the back, just a handshake. And then my partner slipped his hand into mine, quiet as ever, as if nothing extraordinary had happened. He wasn't anticipating thanks or praise; he just had a genuine determination to help another struggling soul.

Watching them together made me realise something. It struck me how many times I had overlooked acts of kindness in favour of seeking my own happiness. Watching him give without reciprocation made me see the light in the happiness that comes from relating to others.

On another occasion during our holiday driving through the countryside, we encountered an unexpected scene: a sheep had escaped from its paddock and stood, trembling on the edge of the highway while cars sped past, its nose bloodied and bruised from trying to find a way through the fence. My heart raced at the thought of danger for both the sheep and those driving by.

Without hesitation my partner pulled over and jumped out of the car. He approached the frightened animal slowly and calmly. At first, irritation bubbled up inside me; I wanted to get to our destination without delay but there was no stopping him now.

For 40 minutes – yes, 40 – I watched as he risked his own safety to gently guide that sheep back through the fence where it belonged. Cars whizzed by dangerously close while he crouched down to say encouraging words to the creature.

When he finally returned to the car with a boyish grin plastered across his face, I saw clearly the pure and unfiltered joy radiating from him, and I couldn't help but soften inside.

In that moment I knew that true happiness comes from sharing kindness. It's not in loud or flashy gestures but in the quiet acts of love that the world becomes just a little softer and kinder.

Because it was not just the sheep he had saved but it was me as well, through this reminder that joy is conceived in small, untimely, inconvenient acts of tenderness.

The unintended consequence of kindness

Those moments resonated with me and, gradually, they changed me.

I was seeking opportunities to give back, not because I thought I 'should', but because it felt right.

At first reaching out to others in small ways felt so insignificant instinctively, I had no idea if my efforts were making a difference or if anyone even saw them. But eventually, that didn't bother me as much and it became about something greater: connection.

A smile and a greeting to a stranger; a kind word to someone who appeared to need it; a moment spent listening instead of passing by and hearing stories of resilience, moments of surprise humour and shared humanity.

With every smile returned, every second of kindness, every thread of connection woven, I found my own happiness deepening, and not the fleeting, airy kind but a more profound, enduring joy anchored in meaning.

That's the secret no one tells you… happiness doesn't run out when you share it; it multiplies.

Why sharing happiness matters

Happiness thrives when shared. It multiplies between us, in a stranger's handshake, in the kindness no one notices, in the giving you do without even expecting something in return.

And the catch is it doesn't take grand gestures to share happiness.

Sometimes it's just sending an encouraging text to a friend who's been quiet lately. Sometimes it's holding the door a little longer, listening without checking your phone or smiling at someone when they look like they might need it.

The smallest acts can create the biggest ripples.

PRACTICAL EXERCISES FOR SPREADING JOY

Here are some ways to bring that ripple into your own life with simple, tangible things you can start today:

1. Happiness ripple map

Draw a map of your world: family, friends, co-workers, neighbours. Around each name, jot down one thing you can do to bring them joy this week. A kind note. A phone call. A shared coffee.

People in my ripple map:	Acts of kindness I can offer:

2. Micro-acts of service

Pick one small act to do each week. Buy coffee for the person behind you in line. Leave a book you love on a park bench with a note inside. Offer to babysit for an exhausted parent.

Ideas for weekly acts of service:

____

____

____

____

3. Legacy letter

Write down how you hope people will feel because of your presence in their lives. Not what you want them to remember you for but how you want them to feel. Warm. Seen. Loved.

My legacy letter:

____

____

____

____

4. Joy projects

Create a 'kindness project'. A kindness jar at work where people drop notes of gratitude. A community clean-up. A monthly dinner where everyone brings food to share with someone in need.

My joy project ideas:

ON A FINAL NOTE

I used to think happiness was a destination, a place I'd one day arrive if I just worked hard enough on myself.

But now I see it differently.

Happiness isn't something you get.

It's something you give.

It's the groceries handed to a stranger; it's the animal rescued on the side of the road; it's lending an ear to someone who needs it.

And the beautiful, unexplainable magic is this: the more happiness you share, the more it comes back, not always from the same person, not always in the same way, but always, somehow, multiplied.

Because joy, unlike almost anything else in life, was never meant to be kept in a closed box. It was meant to be passed on until the world feels just a little lighter, a little softer, a little kinder.

Happiness is a journey, not a destination

Over the course of this book, I've shared pieces of my own story with you not because I've lived perfectly but because I've lived honestly; I've fallen, I've learned and I am still learning. But I wanted to share with anyone, someone, who might be feeling lost like I was and this book might help them find a path to happiness.

So here is what I have learned so far in my journey:

- I learned that rediscovering yourself and peeling away the layers of who the world told you to be is where happiness first whispers.

- I learned that tiny habits can create seismic shifts like a glass of water when you wake up, a gratitude list to remind you of the good that surrounds you or one honest boundary can be the start of everything.

- I learned that happiness sometimes requires forgiveness and release, not to excuse what hurt you but to stop dragging that pain into every tomorrow.

- I learned that you can find purpose beyond pay checks, your worth isn't stamped on your business card and joy doesn't need permission from your title.
- I learned to listen to my body like an ally and not like a machine. To rest without guilt. To view my well-being as the foundation of everything I can offer.
- I learned that resilience isn't about never breaking; it's about rising anyway, even with cracks in your heart.
- I learned that happiness grows when shared through the kindness we offer, the boundaries we uphold, and the sparks of joy we pass from one soul to another.

Every chapter, every reflection, every story was a thread. And together, they wove a single truth:

Happiness isn't something you find.
It's something you practise.

Your invitation

If you're here, you've already taken the first step. You paused. You asked the questions that most people race past:

What does happiness mean to me? How can I bring it into my life, not someday, but now?

But here's the thing: this book is not the end of the road. It's the starting point.

This is your invitation not just to read but to live.

- Take one thing from these pages, just one and weave it into your life today. Maybe it's a gratitude journal.

Maybe it's a morning walk. Maybe it's saying no to something that drains you.

- Then when that feels natural, add another. Then another.

Happiness is built like this, one gentle brick, one honest boundary, one moment of self-love at a time.

Keeping the flame lit

Happiness won't always roar. It won't always be fireworks and laughter. Sometimes it will be quiet like a cup of tea at dawn, a song on the radio that feels like home, a breath that finally feels full after weeks of shallow ones.

Create rituals that remind you to notice it:

- Start your day with one intention.
- Pause at midday for one mindful breath.
- End your evening naming three small things that made you smile.

These aren't just habits. They're protests against numbness. They're invitations to stay awake to your own life.

The big reframe

You will still have setbacks. You will still have days that feel grey. But you'll know now: happiness isn't about avoiding those days.

It's about learning to find a flicker of light in them.

It's about asking, in every moment:

How can I choose joy here? How can I create it? How can I share it?

When you live that way, you stop waiting for happiness to 'arrive' and start living with it.

A parting gift

So, as you close this book, I want to leave you with this:

This isn't a map. It won't tell you every step to take and it was never meant to.

It's a lantern.

It lights the next step. And then the next.

Happiness isn't out there somewhere at the next job, in the next house, in the next version of you.

It's here. In this breath. In this choice. In this moment.

May you stop chasing and start creating.

May you stop waiting and start living.

May you walk lightly, bravely and joyfully.

And may you remember, always:

Happiness isn't a destination. It's the way home.

On the next page is a Happiness Manifesto
that you can tear out or copy to put on your
wall or keep at your desk to remind you every
day that happiness is not a destination.

HAPPINESS MANIFESTO

A simple guide to remind you, every day, that happiness isn't a destination; it's the way you choose to live.

Core principles

- Happiness is not a finish line; it's how you walk.
- Joy is built in small, daily choices and not in one big leap.
- Your body, mind and heart are partners in happiness. Listen to them.
- Boundaries are an act of self-love, not selfishness.
- Abundance grows when you believe there's enough for you and enough to share.
- Happiness multiplies when you give it away.

Daily reminders

- Morning: Set ONE intention for the day.
- Midday: Take a pause with a deep breath, a stretch or a step outside.
- Evening: Name THREE small things that made you smile today.

Affirmations for every day

- I choose joy, even in small ways.
- I create space for peace in my life.
- I am allowed to change, grow and begin again.
- I am the architect of my own happiness.

*Happiness is not a place you arrive; it's
the path you choose every day.*

Carry this manifesto, live it and let it light your way.

REFERENCES

Chapter 2: The science and spirit of happiness

Seligman, M. E. P. (2002). *Authentic happiness: Using the new positive psychology to realise your potential for lasting fulfilment.* New York: Free Press.

Seligman, M. E. P. (2011). *Flourish: A visionary new understanding of happiness and well-being.* New York: Free Press.

Kringelbach, M. L., & Berridge, K. C. (2009). Towards a functional neuroanatomy of pleasure and happiness. *Trends in Cognitive Sciences*, 13(11), 479–487.

Kini, P., Wong, J., McInnis, S., Gabana, N., & Brown, J. W. (2016). The effects of gratitude expression on neural activity. *NeuroImage*, 128, 1–10.

Hölzel, B. K., Carmody, J., Vangel, M., Congleton, C., Yerramsetti, S. M., Gard, T., & Lazar, S. W. (2011). Mindfulness practice leads to increases in regional brain gray matter density. *Psychiatry Research: Neuroimaging*, 191(1), 36–43.

Lazar, S. W., Kerr, C. E., Wasserman, R. H., Gray, J. R., Greve, D. N., Treadway, M. T., & Fischl, B. (2005). Meditation experience is associated with increased cortical thickness. *NeuroReport*, 16(17), 1893–1897.

Lyubomirsky, S., Sheldon, K. M., & Schkade, D. (2005). Pursuing happiness: The architecture of sustainable change. *Review of General Psychology*, 9(2), 111–131.

Lyubomirsky, S. (2007). *The how of happiness: A scientific approach to getting the life you want*. New York: Penguin Books.

Waldinger, R. J., & Schulz, M. S. (2010). What makes for a good life? Lessons from the longest study on happiness. *Psychiatry*, 74(4), 313–329.

Waldinger, R. (2015). *What makes a good life? Lessons from the longest study on happiness*. TED Talk.

Harvard Study of Adult Development. (n.d.). *The longest study of adult life*. Harvard Medical School.

Chapter 5: Habit forming & the power of micro habits

Clear, J. (2018). *Atomic habits: An easy & proven way to build good habits & break bad ones*. New York: Avery.

Fogg, B. J. (2019). *Tiny habits: The small changes that change everything*. Boston: Houghton Mifflin Harcourt.

ABOUT THE AUTHOR

Charu is a business leader, mindset coach, strategist, a writer and a lifelong student of happiness.

After building a successful corporate career she found herself asking some very uncomfortable questions like... *Why don't I feel happy within, when everything on the outside seems "right"? Why do I feel something is off inside me despite all the success professionally and personally?* These questions were the beginning of a personal undoing for her and eventually was the foundation of **The Happiness Pathway.**

Charu's life journey has been shaped by constant healing, resilience and reinvention. Going through periods of profound loss, emotional disruption and rebuilding her life, she learned that happiness is not a destination you arrive at after achieving a milestone or if you are lucky. It is a practice that you build through self-awareness, self-love, boundaries, kindness and intentional daily choices.

Blending personal storytelling with insights from positive psychology, neuroscience, mindset coaching and lived experiences, Charu writes for people who are "doing well" on the outside yet quietly craving more peace, meaning and alignment in their lives. Her work speaks to those who are tired of chasing perfection and ready to build a life that feels authentic, peaceful and their own.

At its core, *The Happiness Pathway* is about remembering who you were before the world told you who to be and choosing to create a life that feels more like home... more YOU.

Charu lives in Australia, where she balances a full professional life with creative work, slow mornings and the belief that happiness doesn't need to be loud to be real.

For permission requests, speaking inquiries or to continue the conversation, you can connect with Charu at *www.thehappinesspathway.com*

@THEHAPPINESSPATHWAY

INSTAGRAM

WWW.THEHAPPINESSPATHWAY.COM

WEBSITE